Harvesting Abundance

LOCAL INITIATIVES OF FOOD AND FAITH

Brian Sellers-Petersen

Foreword by Sarah Nolan

Church Publishing
NEW YORK

To my colleagues at Episcopal Relief & Development, past and present
and
My extended family at St. Mark's Cathedral, Seattle
and
Diocese of Olympia

Unless otherwise noted, the Scripture quotations contained herein are from the New Revised Standard Version Bible, copyright © 1989 by the Division of Christian Education of the National Council of Churches of Christ in the U.S.A. Used by permission. All rights reserved.

Church Publishing
19 East 34th Street
New York, NY 10016
www.churchpublishing.org

Cover image ©Imago Dei Middle School, Tucson, Arizona. Used with permission.
Cover design by Jennifer Kopec, 2Pug Design
Typeset by Rose Design

Library of Congress Cataloging-in-Publication Data

Names: Sellers-Petersen, Brian, author.
Title: Harvesting abundance : local initiatives of food and faith / Brian
 Sellers-Petersen ; foreword by Sarah Nolan.
Description: New York : Church Publishing, 2017.
Identifiers: LCCN 2016057397 (print) | LCCN 2017011595 (ebook) | ISBN
 9780819233103 (ebook) | ISBN 9780819233097 (pbk.)
Subjects: LCSH: Communities—Religious aspects—Christianity. | Community
 gardens. | Food—Religious aspects—Christianity. | Church work—Episcopal
 Church.
Classification: LCC BV625 (ebook) | LCC BV625 .S45 2017 (print) | DDC
 261.8/326—dc23
LC record available at https://lccn.loc.gov/2016057397

Printed in the United States of America

Contents

Foreword

I f you have ever had the opportunity and pleasure of meeting Brian Sellers-Petersen, you quickly learn not only of his extensive interest in church gardens, farms, and food ministries, but of his deep desire to lift up the stories of these ministries and find ways to connect and support the people doing this transformative work. *Harvesting Abundance* is one piece of the legacy that Brian offers all of us in the Episcopal Church, sharing about the lives and stories of the incredible and mundane activities that witness to the Gospel of Jesus, our Baptismal Covenant "to strive for justice and peace among all people," and commitment to the stewardship of all creation.

The first time I met Brian face to face, we talked baseball and chickens. It was spring of 2012, and our farm, The Abundant Table, was one of the early stops for Brian's sabbatical, visiting many of the ministries highlighted in this book. Originating from a campus ministry in the Diocese of Los Angeles, The Abundant Table Farm Project was launched three years prior to Brian's visit, in 2009. With five acres of land, a farm house, and six Episcopal Service Corps young adult interns our little ministry began a very exciting, bumpy, and life changing journey exploring what it means to be reconciled to God, neighbor, and the earth in the ways we worship, work, and live.

Since our first planting of radishes in 2009, The Abundant Table has impacted over 15,000 individuals in Ventura and Los Angeles County through our Farm to School, Farm Education, and Farm to Faith programs. Our worshipping community regularly welcomes groups as small as fifteen and as large as 250 people to various liturgical services, volunteer opportunities, Bible studies, and more.

The Abundant Table strives to "spark a conversation" in the church and the world about the power of growing and sharing food, and the complexity of the associated health and equity issues linked to these processes. We also seek to be a land-based "experiential sanctuary" for the Christian Church, enabling people of faith to find enrichment for their spiritual journey through a land-based encounter with the sacred. We believe renewal of our religious, civic, and ecological communities grows out of the marginal spaces of creativity, resistance and reconciliation.

It is this desire to "spark a conversation" in the wider Episcopal Church, that really brought Brian and I together for more than just a onetime meeting. Brian knows that the growing and sharing of food is an entry point to exploring what it means to care for creation, be concerned about issues of food justice, and practice hospitality. Standing in the backyard of the farmhouse, surrounded by chickens and compost, was the first of what would become many scheming and visioning conversations.

During my time as both an Episcopal Church Foundation Fellow and Episcopal Church Justice and Advocacy Environmental Stewardship Fellow, Brian has been a mentor, connector, and co-conspirator. Over the past five years, we have partnered with an amazing group of individuals all involved in different forms of agrarian ministry and theological work to build the "Cultivate: Episcopal Food Movement," which Brian references in the book's introduction.

Without Brian's tireless work to map the over five hundred farm, garden, and food ministries in the Episcopal Church, the networks and support for these ministries that have been and are developing would not exist in the way they do today. Most of us who are currently part of Cultivate and other similar ministries, all share that we found our way to each other through Brian's doing. Brian knows how much learning we can do from each other, and that the importance of sharing stories and encouraging the church to share more stories is essential to our transformation, renewal and resilience. *Harvesting Abundance* invites us to do just that—learn from each other, be inspired by one another, and witness to the hope and resilience that is planted throughout the Episcopal Church.

> Sarah Nolan
> Director of Programs and Community Partnerships
> The Abundant Table

Acknowledgments

This book grew out of a 2012 sabbatical from working with Episcopal Relief & Development, an organization that has been my occupational home for the past sixteen years. I am particularly grateful to the president, Rob Radtke; the board of directors; and my colleagues and partners for their support and encouragement. Another group that made a large contribution to this book is the founding board of Cultivate: Episcopal Food Movement, especially my cochair, Sarah Nolan. Most importantly I'm grateful for the patience and love of my wife, Pam, and our family.

I am grateful for the scores of gardeners, farmers, beekeepers, organizers, environmentalists, and others involved in faithful food movements who have contributed to this book by giving me tours, subjecting themselves to interviews, taking photos, becoming my e-mail pal, and sharing their stories. First and foremost, I especially give thanks for my editor (friend, encourager, confessor, and cheerleader) at Church Publishing, Sharon Pearson. Thank you Laura Ahrens, Andy Anderson, Devon Anderson, Susan Anderson-Smith, David Bailey, Carol Barnwell, Sarah Bartenstein, Jennifer Baskerville-Burrows, Kathleen Bean, Beth Bojarski, John Burruss, Lauren Carey, George Chlipala, Robin Denncy, Taylor Devine, Pamela Dolan, Jim Eichner, Jim Goodman, Sister Catherine Grace, Ashley Graham-Wilcox, Holly Heine, Cynthia Hizer, Carolyn Hoagland, Bud Holland, Brian Hollstein, J. B. Hoover, Katharine Jefferts Schori, Beth Kelly, Lisa Kimball, Peter Lane, Margaret Larom, Sister Helena Marie, Mark Marshall, Melissa McCarthy, Marilyn McKinney, Alex Montes-Vela, Amanda Musterman, Katie Ong-Landini, Emily Portman, Lisa Ransom, Melissa Rau, Greg Rickel, Peter Rood, Joe Rose, Hunter Ruffin, Leon Sampson, Jim Schaal, Mary Frances Schjonberg, Richard Schori, Bill Slocomb, Rebecca Smith, Kris Stoever, Steve Thomason, Robert Two Bulls, Peter Walsh, Kim Washington, Carolyn White . . .

There are so many more to name. All of you know who you are—my gratitude for your support and inspiration, weeding and harvesting, eating and sharing in abundance.

Introduction

This book is about planting seeds. Instead of broadcasting or sowing seeds of one variety, I'm going with a pollinator seed mix where bees can feast and produce something sweet. If you have ever bought a packet of pollinator seeds, the variety of flowers and blossoms seem endless. The same goes with this book. There are stories and mentions of parish gardens, farms, beehives, hydroponic and aquaponics gardens, sheep tending to a cemetery, and a living labyrinth. My hope is that these stories will continue to help inspire an agrarian movement both inside and outside the Episcopal Church. Through my work with the Food and Faith Initiative of Seattle Tilth, I have been blessed to visit countless gardens of many affiliations in my own backyard of Puget Sound. This book is decidedly parochial since I am spiritually focusing on the Episcopal Church, but you will see that no successful faith-based agrarian ministry does it without partners. The Episcopal Church is just the entry point.

I have been involved in church ministry and international development my whole career. At every point along the way I have had, in the words of the great theologian and philosopher Yogi Berra, "déjà vu all over again" experiences. My current and long-time employer, Episcopal Relief & Development,[1] along with partners throughout the Anglican Communion, have focused a big part of our ministry on alleviating hunger and tackling food insecurity, much of it through small-scale agriculture. My enthusiasm and inspiration come from visits far and wide across the globe as I have seen firsthand the pride and ingenuity of so many people I have encountered along the way.

I was inspired to keep backyard chickens by Don Cornelius and his amazing chicken and egg operation that included a multistory chicken condo/coop in a small village in El Salvador. He told me about being close to absolute despair because he was unable to provide for his family and buy the necessary books and uniforms for his children to go to school. One day an agricultural extension agent working for the Episcopal Diocese of El Salvador and Episcopal Relief &

---

1. *www.episcopalrelief.org.*

Development stopped by, struck up a conversation with Don Cornelius, and after hearing about his situation, kept coming back to listen, learn, and befriend him. After three or four visits, the agent brought Don Cornelius a small box of chicks. This new friend taught Don Cornelius to care for the chicks and eventually helped him to start a chicken and egg business. Don Cornelius was extremely proud that his children were all at school and that he was able to provide jobs to other members of the community.

I have learned new approaches to growing food at home from Episcopal Relief & Development partners: the countless kitchen gardens, school gardens, and farm cooperatives that I have visited in places like Nicaragua, Honduras, Belize, Burundi, South Africa, Cambodia, Brazil, and Ghana. Through the memories of my paternal grandfather and inspiration from a women's beekeeping cooperative in Kenya, I am now the Cathedral apiarist at my home congregation of St. Mark's Cathedral in Seattle. I also work with the Cathedral's urban gardens, which benefit Noel House,[2] a nightly shelter at St. Mark's that cares for women at risk in Seattle.

My interest in agriculture really started at birth: I was born into a family of farmers. While my parents were the first generation to live away from the farm, family farms were not far away. I grew up in small cities and towns that had close connections to agriculture and I lived on the edge of cornfields, literally and figuratively. I spent my summers, vacations, and long weekends at the farms of my grandparents, aunts, and uncles in northeast Nebraska. As a child I gathered eggs, slopped hogs, milked cows, baled hay, and walked up and down rows of corn and beans chopping weeds with a machete. I'm glad my cousins indulged their city cousin. And one indelible summer detassling corn in the Valley of the Jolly Green Giant. End of summer rituals included dressing chickens with my cousins and canning food from my Grandma "Hermer" Tuttle's humongous kitchen garden. My maternal Granddad Tuttle was the stereotypical Midwest farmer. Whenever I see someone in blue-striped overalls, I think of him. He would include me in everything he did, sunup to sundown. He taught me to drive a tractor (John Deere), call hogs (Nebraska style), and fix things with baling wire. He was a great listener and my friend. On the other side of my family, Grandma Petersen was heavy on the Crisco, lived until she was one

---

2. *www.ccsww.org/site/PageServer?pagename=homeless_noelhouse* (accessed December 7, 2016).

hundred years old, and taught me how to cook. My paternal grandfather was an agricultural entrepreneur—he owned and managed two farms, sold DeKalb seeds, was a buyer for a Midwest wool company, and was the local State Farm insurance agent. My most vivid memory of my Grandpa Petersen was of him in his black suit, shiny black shoes, and horn-rimmed glasses going out to check the beehives in-between his other jobs.

Why Church Gardens?

The Bible and Jesus's teachings are full of agrarian stories, metaphors, and parables. In the beginning, God created a garden. As we read in Genesis 2:8–9, within that garden God placed humankind to tend and care for it. Thousands of years later, Jesus told parables about seeds, soil, and abundance. While Jesus learned carpentry from Joseph, farming was most likely a central part of his family life, as most people in Israel were subsistence farmers at the time. Almost always, Jesus's first point of reference was growing food for sustenance; hence his stories feature a sower, a mustard seed, fig trees, vines, and harvests. Paul carried that message forward in his letters:

> And God is able to provide you with every blessing in abundance, so that by always having enough of everything, you may share abundantly in every good work. As it is written,
>
> > "He scatters abroad, he gives to the poor;
> > his righteousness endures forever."
>
> He who supplies seed to the sower and bread for food will supply and multiply your seed for sowing and increase the harvest of your righteousness. (2 Cor. 9:8–10)

We have a never-ending list of reasons to be involved in agricultural ministries as a church. For starters, our Baptismal Covenant calls us to proclaim by word and example the Good News of God in Christ; to seek and serve Christ in all persons, loving our neighbor as ourselves; and to strive for justice and peace among all people, respecting the dignity of every human being.[3] Involvement

---

3. The Book of Common Prayer (New York: Church Publishing, 1979), 304–5.

in a variety of food and agricultural ministries can be found in each of the Five Marks of Mission:

- To proclaim the Good News of the Kingdom
- To teach, baptize, and nurture new believers
- To respond to human need by loving service
- To transform unjust structures of society, to challenge violence of every kind, and pursue peace and reconciliation
- To strive to safeguard the integrity of creation, and sustain and renew the life of the earth[4]

For me, the bottom line and raison d'etre is Genesis 2:15: "The Lord God took the man and put him in the Garden of Eden to till it and keep (tend) it."

This book is also an outgrowth of another biblical concept: Jubilee and the sabbath year. Sabbath rest is first mentioned in Genesis 2:2–3 and other passages. Deuteronomy 5:12–15 calls for a rest after six days of work. Sabbatical year or *shmita* (literally "release") is commanded in Leviticus 25 to desist from working the fields during the seventh year. Jubilee comes at the end of seven cycles of *shmita,* or forty-nine years. Jubilee deals largely with land, property, and property rights. According to Leviticus, slaves and prisoners would be freed, debts would be forgiven, and the mercies of God would be particularly manifested. Much of Sabbath is tied to the land.

We can think of these concepts as theologies of work as well as rest. In 2012 I took a working sabbatical. I looked at countless examples of agricultural work in the Episcopal Church, discovering the similarities to agricultural ministry throughout the Anglican Communion, especially in the areas of alleviating hunger, climate change resistant farming, and food security. I began mapping the Episcopal Church congregations, camps and conference centers, schools, seminaries, monasteries, and more who were engaged in agricultural and related food ministries. Most of this work has been merged into the Episcopal Asset Map,[5] a joint project of Episcopal Relief & Development and the Domestic Poverty Office of the Episcopal Church. It is also chronicled on the

---

4. *http://www.episcopalchurch.org/page/five-marks-mission.*

5. *https://episcopalassetmap.org.*

Cultivate: Episcopal Food Movement Facebook page.[6] I am grateful to the School of Theology at the University of the South for providing me with a fellowship to start work on what follows.

It is important for us to give our land a rest, to have a sabbatical. Metaphorically and physically, we need to take a break from gardening or farming to spend time building the soil. I remember my Granddad Tuttle "fallowing" sections of his farmland. Instead of growing crops, he let his livestock eat from it and poop on it before putting it back into crop production. It is where we get the term "dung a tree." He also practiced crop rotation and took advantage of what he referred to as government acres, in which farmers were paid not to grow crops.[7]

I have come to believe that we need to consider fallowing our ministries, instead of keeping them on life support: to pause and regroup; to decide if maybe we are being called to another ministry. Perhaps our gardens can teach us about living out our faith while caring for our spiritual as well as physical lives. The ground must lay fallow for a season to enable it to produce a crop. When treating fallow soil, it is important to till mulch (decomposed organic material) into it to enrich it. Proper mulching requires that the organic material be regularly turned. This turning allows the old material to decompose and become a rich, dark material, from which the roots of the plants can obtain the necessary nutrients. This tilling of decomposed organic material represents us dying to the things of the world and allowing God to make our weaknesses into our strengths. Wisdom is the nutrient of healthy soil, learning from our mistakes. Yes, the garden can teach us a lot.

Gleaning also figures prominently in the Old Testament:

> When you reap the harvest of your land, you shall not reap to the very edges of your field, or gather the gleanings of your harvest; you shall leave them for the poor and for the alien: I am the LORD your God. (Lev. 23:22)

Today's foraging ministry is another aspect of agricultural initiatives in many church gardens today. Food grown is given to food pantries, soup kitchens,

---

6. *https://www.facebook.com/EpiscopalFoodMovement/?fref=ts.*

7. That concept is beyond the range of this book, but you can learn more here: *http://www.pbs.org/newshour/making-sense/why-does-the-govt-pay-farmers/* (accessed November 16, 2016).

and neighborhoods located in food deserts. In 1979 the Society of Saint Andrew[8] was formed in Virginia as an intentional community of two Methodist families called to life and ministry together in Christ. It has grown into an ecumenical, nonprofit charitable organization whose mission is to introduce people to God's grace in Jesus Christ through meeting their hungers by gleaning—salvaging fresh, nutritious produce from American farms that otherwise would be left to rot—and delivering it to agencies across the country. Another exciting and tasty example of a food ministry I learned about was a recent dinner that consisted of gathered, hunted, fished, or grown food by congregation members and friends at St. Andrew's Parish in Aberdeen, Washington. I think they are on to something, and I suspect there are dozens of other faith communities that are doing the same.

The Power of Stories

This is a book of stories. We shouldn't have to be convinced about the theological soundness or importance of agricultural and environmental stewardship ministries. But in hearing others' stories, we can be changed. Within these pages are stories of church ministries that are focused on growing food for our tables and flowers for our altars. But there are also stories of livestock, bees, farmers' markets, and a wide variety of food ministries. There are hundreds if not thousands of church gardens with food and agricultural ministries throughout the Episcopal Church. They are not always easy to find; I dare say many church gardeners and farmers "hide their light under a bushel." The best way to find where these ministries are happening is by word of mouth. If you tell a story about your parish (school, seminary . . .) garden or beehives or food ministry, you will invariably be told about another. This book focuses on at least thirty food and faith stories, with plenty more sprinkled throughout.

The story of gardening in the Episcopal Church goes back to precolonial times. One tradition that has been lost is the concept of the glebe. According to Merriam-Webster, it is "land belonging or yielding revenue to a parish church or ecclesiastical benefice." Since the Church of England was the established church of Great Britain, glebe land was distributed by the colonial government

---

8. *http://endhunger.org/about-sosa/.*

before we became the United States and was often farmed or rented out by the church priest to cover his living expenses. A good example is Glebe Church,[9] an Episcopal congregation in Suffolk, Virginia. The Glebe House in Woodbury, Connecticut is now an historic house museum and garden. Once a parsonage, its history is connected to the election of Bishop Samuel Seabury as the first American Episcopal bishop.[10] Today we see the word on street signs in states like Maryland and Virginia. Most of us don't realize that these are connected to the Episcopal and Anglican Church.

What if we resurrected this concept—at least as far as better utilizing the land that we have? The Episcopal Church owns a lot of land! Some of the land we own is pre–Revolutionary War titled property that generations of stewards have refused to sell off to developers. Some come from bequests that in turn are used as rental properties with income that supports a variety of ministries. Through my work and sabbatical I now look at church land assets in a completely different way. I see edible gardens and landscaping on a variety of church property: congregations, schools, seminaries, monasteries, camps and conference centers, diocesan offices . . . some large and some small, in containers and on acres of adjacent land. I have even seen and heard about indoor hydroponic gardens, roof gardens, beehives, and an aquaponic garden on a church parking lot. Can you envision all the underutilized tracts of church land with all sorts of potential now being used? I often wonder how much time and money we spend on maintaining grassy lawns that might only be used for the annual Easter egg hunt and Pentecost picnic.

More and more young people are discerning a call to Holy Orders or a lay vocation that includes farming as a part of their ministry. With the amount of land that is sitting unused, I think we need to start exploring how we can support more agricultural ministry. It is exciting to see the University of the South, which used to require all students to work on their farm, reviving their agricultural heritage through the University Farm that is growing crops and bringing back livestock. One of my favorite examples of creativity, ingenuity, and making use of available space or lack thereof is Imago Dei Middle School in Tucson, Arizona, that doesn't have a stitch of soil. What it does have is a concrete courtyard

---

9. *http://glebechurch.org/GlebeHistory1.htm.*

10. *http://www.glebehousemuseum.org/about_us.*

that has been transformed into urban oasis using horse troughs, containers, and a one-of-a-kind vertical garden. Virginia Theological Seminary and Episcopal High School in Alexandria have almost two hundred acres between them with gardens, greenhouses, beehives, and more plans for the future. All Saints Church and their First Nations' Kitchen in Minneapolis has brought traditional food to residents of the nearby Little Earth of the United Tribes, the largest indigenous urban housing community in the United States. With the help of a United Thank Offering (UTO) grant, they now grow "The Three Sisters" (corn, squash, and beans) using heirloom seeds. This practice is starting to be used at parishes in other parts of the United States. The Diocese of Los Angeles Diocesan Center at the Cathedral of St. Paul now has a living and edible labyrinth[11] where one can internally feed one's soul while externally food is being grown for feeding the body.

Everyone Can Do Something

One of my fondest memories was visiting a church garden that had a raised bed built on a concrete pad, high enough for someone to sit in a wheelchair and get their hands in the dirt. It also had a sturdy wooden box for a young child to stand on. While I was there I watched an unlikely duo of an older woman and little boy, about six years old, working side by side. The boy was jabbering away, with the woman giving him instructions when she could get a word in edgewise. It was a picture of intergenerational connection.

If there are those in your congregation not eager to literally get their hands dirty, there are other ways to support this ministry. During a short two-year interval between working at a parish and a very large NGO, I was the California regional organizer of Bread for World.[12] Art Simon, its founder, was committed to the idea that sending a letter to your member of Congress could change a life.

Be an advocate. What percentage of your local school lunch programs includes local fresh food? Check with your school district and if you think it is too low, do something about it. Better food policies means healthier children who grow up to be full citizens. Today it is exciting to see farmers' markets

---

11. *http://seedsofhope.ladiocese.org/living-labyrinth.html.*
12. *www.bread.org.*

including markets hosted by churches accepting SNAP (food stamps) or WIC (Women, Infants, and Children Food and Nutrition Service) benefits. Learn more about the US Farm Bill. Every few years one of the most consequential pieces of legislation finds its way through the United States Congress to the president's desk. It impacts not just US farmers and agribusiness, but programs like the Mississippi River Basin Healthy Watersheds Initiative and Ogallala Aquifer Initiative, the USDA's Local Food Promotion Program and School Summer Food Service Program, the Agency for International Development's (USAID) Feed the Future program, and Helping Address Rural Vulnerabilities and Ecosystem Stability program (HARVEST).

Local advocacy makes a difference. In my hometown of Seattle, a model for other towns and cities across the United States, there has been a proliferation of city P-Patches, known as community gardens in most other places. Through the active involvement of citizen groups, a $146 million parks and green space levy was passed with $2 million going to the development of an additional twenty-eight P-Patch gardens. Today eighty-eight P-Patches are distributed throughout the city. Community gardeners grow food on 14.9 acres of the land and in addition steward 18.8 acres for the public for a total of 32 acres.[13]

Think beyond the Work

Gardens are also evangelism tools. One reason to have a garden on the church's front lawn or most visible site is that it will receive lots of foot traffic. You might not initially get many fans from those who are used to lovely ornamental landscaping, but with some care and thought, you can win them over with a carefully designed array of purple basil, rainbow chard, intercropped flowers, fruit trees, and *fill in the blank*. And think about how your garden can smell if you include a variety of herbs. If people walk past your garden on a regular basis, you are going to be motivated to keep it weeded and looking good. It's going to communicate to members, neighbors, and visitors your values and how we are a people of faith committed to gathering around a table to eat.

---

13. *http://www.seattle.gov/neighborhoods/programs-and-services/p-patch-community-gardening/about-the-p-patch-program/parks-and-green-space-levy.*

In addition to the human kind, vegetables and herbs present a hospitable environment for productive visitors such as butterflies, bees, and earthworms. The traditional floral components of our front landscape undoubtedly benefit from all these happy and busy critters. It is part of our environmental stewardship. As we cultivate the soil, we care for the earth and promote discipleship. Church agriculture is one of the ways to mitigate climate change. Is there a way to figure out carbon offset through growing food on our properties and composting our food waste and other compostable materials, instead of sending it to the dump or having a composting service pick our waste up in a big fossil fuel–burning truck?

Gardening is formational. As a part of the team that developed Episcopal Relief & Development's Abundant Life Garden Project® program, I frequently say that everything you really need to know about God you can learn in a garden. The garden teaches forgiveness. To make sure that you pull weeds. At the end of the gardening season, you can pile seemingly dead plants in a compost bin, only to come back in the spring and find it teaming with worms and other vital materials that will help your new garden spring back to life.

Sources of Inspiration

I have a couple of go-to places and people to connect with when I need a shot in the arm, such as when I turn my back and a whole row of lettuce has gone to seed, or when a critter comes for an extended snack time, or when the hoped-for group of volunteers don't materialize. Ron Finley, the guerrilla gardener of Los Angeles, provides inspiration and much-needed humor. His TED talk and 2014 presentation to the Episcopal Church Building Fund can be found online.[14] The Holy Family of Jesus Cambodian Church of Tacoma's community garden is a short drive from my house. I like to just sit in the middle of the garden and enjoy the peace. It has been around for almost twenty years with a wild and organized beauty that never fails to grab my heart. At St. Mark's Cathedral, Seattle, I love watching the rooftop beehives; one of the most amazing creatures in God's creation comes and goes, dances, and points their fellow

---

14. *https://www.ted.com/talks/ron_finley_a_guerilla_gardener_in_south_central_la.*

workers to where the food is. The Cascade P-Patch Community Garden where my friend Dick Blount used to have a plot; his spirit and love of life is incarnated in the people, plants, and food in the shadow of REI's (a well-known national retailer based in Seattle) headquarters and I-5 that runs through Seattle. Find the people and places near you that give you inspiration.

The Abundance before Us

My personal guiding light is St. Benedict and the theology of *ora et labora* (prayer and work), or as my former boss at All Saints, Pasadena, George Regas, would say, "Prayer is in the work." The Benedictines and Cistercians applied *ora et labora* directly to farm work and the development of a movement toward land reclamation and agricultural development.

New initiatives of agricultural and environmental stewardship are almost too many to list and their stories are really without end. In addition to the stories shared within this book, I commend to you: Abundant Table Farm, Plainsong Farm, the Diocese of Los Angeles's Seeds of Hope, Sustainable Ministries of Western Tennessee, the Church and Community Gardens of the Diocese of Rochester, Bellwether Farm, and Thistle Farms. There are many people and places to seek out to be inspired, get counsel, and learn.

In terms of the Episcopal Church, foremost among them, is Cultivate: Episcopal Food Movement. Cultivate is a grassroots network of people involved in agrarian ministries in the Episcopal Church. It is committed to building and strengthening a network that engages with the Episcopal Church to discover how agrarian work can transform our culture, our institutions, our environment, and ourselves through gardens, farms, and conservation. The work of Cultivate is to create a just and sustainable food system, which reflects the abundance and grace of God. To find Cultivate, go to *https://www.facebook. com/EpiscopalFoodMovement/*.

If you need some theological convincing, I would start and end with Wendell Berry, who states, "Eating is an agricultural act."[15] In-between I would include Fred Bahnson, Ellen Davis, Sara Miles, Ched Myers, Ragan Sutterfield,

---

15. *https://www.ecoliteracy.org/article/wendell-berry-pleasures-eating* (accessed November 16, 2016).

and Norman Wirzba, (check out the resources in Appendix E on page 150). My real hope is that you look to those who have their hands in the dirt—the farmers, gardeners, and all engaged in food ministries—as the practical theologians who have a story to share.

After you have read this book, a good place to continue your search for ideas and inspiration is the Episcopal Church Asset Map, developed by Episcopal Relief & Development and The Episcopal Church. All you need to do is click the Community Garden button at www.episcopalassetmap.org. My prayer and hope is that this little book can help us share those stories of agricultural ministry, of prayer and work, being lived out by Episcopal churches that show how we can be better stewards of the land that God has entrusted to us.

> He also said, "With what can we compare the kingdom of God, or what parable will we use for it? It is like a mustard seed, which, when sown upon the ground, is the smallest of all the seeds on earth; yet when it is sown it grows up and becomes the greatest of all shrubs, and puts forth large branches, so that the birds of the air can make nests in its shade." (Mark 4:30–32)

"Digging Deep" at Camp Stevens, Julian, California. (*Photo courtesy of Ashley Graham-Wilcox. Used with permission.*)

1

Environmental Change-Makers and the Community Garden
Holy Nativity, Westchester, California

stablished during World War II as a place for the burgeoning neighborhood to gather on Sundays for family worship, Holy Nativity is located
on the west side of Los Angeles. In 1947 homes cost $6,000, while
today they sell for $950,000. Originally agreements in the planned community
prevented homeowners from growing their own food or cultivating gardens,
as these practices might compete against local farmers.[1] Once an agricultural
area, it is now a hub for air travel; Los Angeles International Airport is its neighbor. Times have changed along with the landscape, and Holy Nativity has
responded to those changes.

As with churches in many urban areas, there was a growing concern about
food insecurity within Los Angeles County. Holy Nativity had a sizeable piece
of land surrounding the church, so leaders began to wonder if the conventional
landscaping of juniper bushes and green lawn could be turned into edible landscaping. What if a community garden could be established that would provide
produce to the local food pantry? With vestry approval in 2008, people from
churches, mosques, and synagogues; community volunteers; and Holy Nativity
parishioners dug up 1,100 square feet of property and created a vegetable garden.

Since then the original garden has grown to four thousand square feet
and expanded to include twenty-six fruit trees, a medicinal herb garden, and a

---

1. Many of the details of Holy Trinity's gardens and Change-Makers was shared by Peter Rood at a workshop
during Virginia Theological Seminary's annual fall convocation on October 5, 2016, in Alexandria, Virginia.

wildflower garden that attracts bees and butterflies. The garden is maintained by a team comprised of local neighbors, food activists, social justice activists, and people who just like to garden. The team gathers every Thursday from late afternoon until dusk to work in the garden. The bounty is delivered to the Food Pantry LAX for distribution throughout the wider community.

> **Seeds of Hope** A ministry of the Episcopal Diocese of Los Angeles that seeks to help congregations, communities, and schools turn unused land into productive gardens and orchards to provide healthy and fresh food in areas of need across the county.

The Community Garden is not all that Holy Nativity offers on the environmental front. Environmental Change-Makers (ECM) began in 2005 when five local neighbors met with the rector, Peter Rood, in the Holy Nativity Community Hall to decide what they could possibly do about ecological problems like global warming. From these humble beginnings ECM grew, and as the members discussed individual triumphs in "doing something" to help the environment, they began hosting events such as movies and talks with guest speakers.

ECM was incorporated in 2012 as a California nonprofit corporation and is in the process of applying for 501(c)(3) tax-exempt status. Today it is a joint project under the direction of Joanne Poyourow (who designed the garden as well as other local gardens and manages its plantings) and John Tikotsky (a landscape architect who designed the rainwater harvesting for the garden), along with Peter Rood.

Through ECM, organic vegetable garden classes are taught each month, open to the general public. Topics have included planning an autumn vegetable garden, crop rotations, attracting good bugs, and water wisdom. Joanne has also written several booklets and how-to guides, which are sold to the community gardeners.

The gardens at Holy Nativity have been a catalyst for change in the community. Where once gardens were prohibited, now they thrive, making a space for sharing environmental solutions. The gates to the gardens are pieces of art that remain open for any and all to walk in and experience the wonder of creation. At the Change-Makers' monthly meetings they seek new ideas, share with one another, model changes, and show others that through everyday living environmental sustainability is possible.

Emerson Avenue Community Garden Just a few blocks from Holy Nativity is Orville Wright Middle School. An adjacent abandoned one-acre property was once the site of agricultural programs in the 1970s. Working with local city officials and a local teacher in 2009, the Environmental Change-Makers of Holy Nativity helped bring this garden back to life. The garden is being built by volunteer labor. One section of the space is a school garden with plots for classes. Another section will eventually have traditional community garden plots. Additional features include a native plants garden to attract native pollinators and other "good bugs," an urbanite and cob outdoor classroom, a mini-orchard of fruit trees, and a one-fifth mile walking track.

"Giant Beets" at Imago Dei Middle School (*Photo courtesy of Anne Sawyer. Used with permission.*)

2

Hunger No More Urban Garden
Imago Dei Middle School, Tucson, Arizona

Founded by Episcopal priests Anne Sawyer and Susan Anderson-Smith, Imago Dei Middle School is an independent, Episcopal, tuition-free middle school serving low-income families in Tucson. Dependent on charitable donations from hundreds of individuals, businesses, and foundations who share a vision of breaking the cycle of poverty through quality education, Imago Dei is a success story on how a school can grow an urban garden and engage students at the same time.

Susan Anderson-Smith, chaplain of Imago Dei, became concerned about the physical health of her students while observing their eating habits and listening to their stories about what kinds of food they ate with their families. Using the program *What's on Your Plate?*[1] teachers and students began working on the activities in the workbook. One of the activities was to draw a picture of their neighborhood, designating the location of libraries, playgrounds, grocery stores, schools, and so forth. In the process, Susan learned that *no* child in the class lived in a neighborhood that had any source of food better than a convenience store. After doing research, she learned more about healthy, reliable, organic, sustainable, affordable food—and how it was not available to most of the families who attended Imago Dei. Thus began Hunger No More Urban Garden, as they learned how to grow their own food through creating an urban organic garden in the limited space behind the school in the hope that what was learned would be taken back into the children's neighborhoods.

---

1. *www.whatsonyourplateproject.org.*

The students—the scholars—became engaged and empowered. They became self-determined about their garden as well as their health and wholeness. Susan shares how "it is a joy to watch their joy in creating and caring for the garden, and in the food it produces. They are becoming advocates for themselves and their communities for reliable and healthy food sources as well as healthy and humane production of food."[2]

It wasn't easy. They faced numerous hurdles: getting middle schoolers interested in growing and eating anything that might be healthy can be a challenge. Getting them to remember to water can be another frustration, as can growing anything in the desert. A limited growing season and a lack of water can be obstacles, but there are always solutions. With time, the students began to connect the dots.

Today the garden serves many purposes in addition to growing vegetables. Yes, it is a laboratory for the school's scholars to learn why and how to grow healthy food, but it also helps them learn how to run a small business. Seedlings are sold at local farmers' markets, with proceeds used to acquire seeds and other gardening materials. The food grown is now used to supplement the school lunches and snacks. Families who are in greatest need also receive produce from the harvest.

It is not just about growing vegetables and flowers. In the process of becoming gardeners, scholars learned about the whole food growth cycle, including the vital role that bees play through pollination. A potter now makes available beautifully handmade pottery bee pots; the students plant flowers in them (knowing that gardeners love growing flowers to attract pollinators) and also sell them at farmers' markets.

Partnerships have been important to the success of this program, with Intuit becoming a main partner. Susan shares that through a mutual friend, a member of Intuit's "Innovation Catalyst" team was "cultivated" and has organized more than fifty employees over the years to come to the school to teach the scholars how to run a small business. They have learned life skills such as how to: develop a budget; keep track of inventory, sales, and profits; market and sell; calculate the cost of production; develop and sell new products; and even develop and deliver an elevator speech.

---

2. Susan Anderson-Smith, e-mail correspondence with author, June 30, 2016.

School gardens provide outdoor learning laboratories for children to experiment. They improve children's health by expanding the variety and quantity of fruits and vegetables they consume. They even offer a chance to learn math in a hands-on way by weighing and measuring produce. Many Episcopal schools include gardening and agriculture as part of their curriculum. Some examples include: The Episcopal School of Knoxville has a butterfly garden, a chicken coop and offers an agriculture and sustainability class in the third through fifth grades. The Gooden School in Sierra Madre, California, has a Garden of Hope, and St. Margaret's School in San Juan Capistrano, California, has a school-wide garden and greenhouse with preschool and lower school satellite gardens. Iolani School, Honolulu, and St. Hilda and St. Hugh School, New York City, both have roof gardens. Trinity Episcopal School in Charlotte, North Carolina, is part of the Green Teacher Network that offers workshops and support to teachers and volunteers. St. Mathew's School, Pacific Palisades, in the Diocese of Los Angeles has a "food" partnership with the St. Paul's School, Caracol, in the Diocese of Haiti.[3]

Other partners have included master gardeners, community garden individuals, and University of Arizona experts who have helped the school learn about composting and water harvesting. One remarkable feature of the garden is a vertical garden on a wrought iron fence on one of the sides of the garden (the other three sides are made up of brick buildings). It is made up of a series of old pairs of blue jeans with the legs cut off and sewn up above the knee. The legs are filled up with small stones and gravel to help with drainage and topped with soil and compost, with tomatoes spilling out the top.

In addition to being the cofounder and chaplain at Imago Dei, Susan has strong connections to gardening. She reflects:

How far we have removed ourselves from the earth and living simply and responsibly, all in the name of convenience and efficiency and modernity. My maternal grandparents, their sisters, and brothers were all farmers, not as a business, but as a way of life. I spent many summers helping my grandparents and my great aunts

---

3. *http://www.episcopalrelief.org/what-you-can-do/act/friends-of-episcopal-relief-and-development?story=from-our-kitchen-to-their-kitchen-california-school-reaches-out.*

and uncles harvest crops and can vegetables so we would all have something to eat in the winter. I knew which fruits and vegetables were in season when, and when they weren't in season, you didn't eat them. I have been reconnected with these memories and have been compelled to look at how I can personally live more simply so others may simply live, as well as promote that thinking and behavior in our scholars.[4]

Imago Dei offers their middle school students a chance to participate in long-term projects that give back to the community and to the planet. Through water-harvesting, building and maintaining an organic garden, raising and selling organic seedling vegetables and bee-attractive plants at a farmers' market, they effect real change in a world while learning about social and environmental issues.

Escuela Agricola Hogar de Amor y Esperanza / **The Agricultural School and Farm** Located one hour outside of Tegucigalpa in Talanga, Honduras, the Agricultural School is home to over sixty boys in grades seven to nine. The 240-acre farm sits in a quiet and pastoral setting, with views of rolling mountains. Under the supervision of Director Yoni Aguilera, the boys study sustainable agriculture. Days begin very early—usually before 5 a.m. The boys spend their mornings doing their farm chores and attending workshops, while the afternoons are spent in academic classes. Students focus their studies on either plant and crop production or animal care. In crop production, they learn relevant farming techniques, such as terrace farming, drip irrigation, and crop rotation. In animal care, the boys work with chickens, goats, sheep, pigs, cows, and tilapia. Fresh food raised at the school helps to feed students at all four El Hogar campuses. The campus also includes acres of beans, corn, greens, bananas, mangos, and other vegetables and fruits. After graduation, some continue on with their education or get jobs, and others go back to their own communities to teach sustainable principles to other local farmers.

---

4. Susan Anderson-Smith, e-mail correspondence with author, July 26, 2016.

"Market Table" at St. Michael's & All Angels' Farmers Market in Dallas (*Photo courtesy of Hunter Ruffin. Used with permission.*)

Farmers' Markets
Church Parking Lots

I n its simplest form, according to Wikipedia, "a farmers' market (also farmers market) is a physical retail market featuring foods sold directly by farmers to consumers."[1] Pretty simple, but after checking out lots of farmers' markets hosted or sponsored by Episcopal congregations, the definition should include the making of personal connections between farmers, shoppers, congregations, and communities for the mutual benefit of all. If you have a parking lot or front lawn, access to farmers who need their food sold, people who eat, and a creative group ready to roll up their sleeves, you can start a farmers' market ministry. There are hundreds of church-based farmers' markets that you can go to for inspiration and advice. Here are a few stories, excuse the pun, gleaned from their websites (of which the links are listed in Appendix D).

The Healthier Heart Farmer's Market
Trinity Episcopal Cathedral, Trenton, New Jersey

The Healthier Heart Farmer's Market at Trinity makes healthy and fresh produce available to our urban neighbors through the participation of regional farmers who accept cash; EBT cards; Women, Infants, and Children (WIC) benefits; and Senior Farmers' Market vouchers. Generally open each Friday throughout the summer, the market also partners with local hospitals and community-based organizations to offer complimentary health screenings and

---

1. *Wikipedia*, s.v. "Farmers' Market," last modified December 29. 2016, *https://en.wikipedia.org/wiki/Farmers'_market*.

educational materials. Through cooperation with the Mercer County Office of Aging and Nutrition, the market is also a convenient distribution site for Senior Farmers' Market vouchers, a program that allows eligible seniors to receive financial assistance for the purchase of Jersey Fresh fruits and vegetables. To further the cathedral's mission of fellowship and hospitality, all visitors to the market are served a free nutritious lunch made from local produce, with opportunities to attend regularly scheduled "healthier eating" educational workshops, cooking classes, Bible study, and organized prayer.[2]

Peachtree Road Farmers' Market
Cathedral of St. Philip, Atlanta, Georgia

Now in its tenth year, Peachtree Road Farmers' Market is a leader in the community, being the largest producer-only farmers' market in the state. Producer-only means that everything at the market has been grown, raised, or made by the seller, ensuring fair prices for both the vendors and the consumers. The market takes place on Saturday mornings beginning early April until mid-December and Wednesday evenings mid-April to the end of October. The market is open rain or shine; in the event of bad weather, the entire market is moved inside the Cathedral of St. Philip. Both of our markets accept SNAP (food stamps / can process EBT cards) and double the dollar value. There are fifty weekly vendors and over thirty-five chef demonstrations are held through the season. Each week brings new produce, vendors, events, live music, and fun! On Wednesday evenings, guest can enjoy farm-to-table fresh meals on site or to take home. Live music, chef pop-ups, and local breweries make it the perfect evening for gathering as a community.[3]

Farmers Market
St. Stephen's, Richmond, Virginia

The mission of the Farmers Market at St. Stephen's is to seek "to connect our choices about the foods we buy and eat to our call to be stewards of God's

---

2. *www.trinitycathedralnj.org/the-healthier-heart-farmers-market.html.*

3. *www.peachtreeroadfarmersmarket.com.*

creation, as we build community and support local farmers." Their goals include: "connecting God's call to environmental stewardship to the foods we eat, stewardship of resources, and reducing the carbon footprint of what we eat; building community by providing the city of Richmond and our local neighborhood with a healthy way to gather and connect with each other on a regular basis; educating patrons with practical ways to maintain the connection with the sources of their food; and helping fill the growing demand for fresh, locally grown and prepared foods in Richmond."[4] Patrons can speak directly to the people who grow and produce the food, learn what methods and practices the farmer or producer uses, and get tips about how to prepare the produce, eggs, meat, poultry, and other goodies offered. Many customers remark on the size of the market: it's big enough to have what they need, but it's not overwhelming. Free parking is available and children, bicycles, and dogs are welcome.

Greene Street Market
Church of the Nativity, Huntsville, Alabama

The Greene Street Market at Nativity is downtown Huntsville's producer-only, open-air market for fresh, locally grown vegetables, fruits, herbs, and flowers. You can meet farmers with gorgeous local produce, grass fed beef and pork, free range chickens, and eggs; pick up freshly prepared meals, gourmet popsicles, traditionally made relishes, cheeses, preserves, and breads. Open Thursdays from May to October, local artisans also offer their works alongside vendors who sell prepared foods in addition to the fresh food.[5]

Saint Michael's Farmers Market
Saint Michael and All Angels, Dallas, Texas

The Saint Michael's Farmers Market is a nonprofit community outreach ministry of Saint Michael and All Angels Episcopal Church where local farmers, ranchers, and artisans sell directly to the North Dallas neighborhood. The

---

4. *http://www.ststephensrva.org/community/farmers-market/*.

5. *www.greenestreetmarket.com*.

market's focus is on local food, with food vendors required to sell at least 60 percent of their own homegrown products. Products must come from within 150 miles of Dallas County. The producers' growing practices vary. Some vendors do have farming practices that are chemical-free and pesticide-free, commonly known as naturally grown or possibly USDA certified organic.[6]

Homegrown Alabama Farmers Market
Canterbury Episcopal Chapel, Tuscaloosa, Alabama

Homegrown Alabama is a student-led group at the University of Alabama that seeks to educate students about the value of local produce, as well as to foster partnerships between local farmers and the University of Alabama. Partners include Canterbury Episcopal Chapel, Alabama Farmers Market Authority, UA Office of Community Affairs, Students for Sustainability, and the SGA

> **The Episcopal Farmworker Ministry** (EFwM), a joint ministry between the Diocese of East Carolina and North Carolina, has been serving farmworkers in Johnston, Harnett, and Sampson Counties in eastern North Carolina for nearly three decades. Farmworkers play a vital role in cultivating the food we eat every day, and North Carolina has one of the largest farmworker populations in the nation. Even though 85 percent of our fruits and vegetables are harvested by hand, farmworkers remain largely invisible. Despite their essential role in feeding our nation, they are often mistreated and abused by employers and face a multitude of barriers that keep them from ensuring even the most basic of living standards. EFwM ministers to 3,500 farmworkers each growing season by proving Spanish-language sacramental ministries and Eucharist celebrations. Some of the programmatic ministries include immigration assistance; transportation services; food, clothing, and toiletry kit collection and distribution; labor camp visits; counseling; and English as a Second Language (ESL classes), as well as a visitors program for church, community, and school groups. No one is denied services based on ability to pay. See *http://efwm.dionc.org.*

---

6. *http://www.saintmichaelsmarket.com/.*

Department of Environmental Concerns. The goal at Homegrown Alabama is to facilitate relationships between local growers and the community they feed. As well as a food ministry, it is also a teaching ministry for students and the community to learn that what we put on our plates is being grown in ways to improve the health of the soil, so animals and plants can continue to be productive for our grandchildren's grandchildren. They advocate eating fruits and vegetables in season because they're fresher, healthier, and far tastier, and the variety keeps eating interesting.

Discover more farmers' markets in Appendix D on pages 145–150.

"A Rainbow of Lettuces" at Bluestone Farm (*Photo courtesy of Community of the Holy Spirit. Used with permission.*)

4

Shepherd Farm

Church of the Good Shepherd, Town and Country, Missouri

A growing suburban St. Louis parish realized in 2013 that they had five acres of land that was simply growing grass. While the children in the congregation were exploring God's creation using Episcopal Relief & Development's Abundant Life Garden Project® program in their Christian formation classes, other members of the congregation were having conversations about hunger and food insecurity in and around St. Louis. The Holy Spirit brought these groups together, and with an anonymous gift of $10,000 for start-up costs, a group of committed volunteers stepped forward. With those two important ingredients financial and human resources—ground was turned for the first time in March 2014 and Shepherd Farm was born.

When starting the garden, the goal was to give produce weekly to a program in St. Louis called the Peace Meal. The garden/farm is 30 x 90 feet and harvested 2,000 pounds of food the first year and approximately 2,200 pound the second year. The year 2016 marked their third growing season. Today the vegetables and herbs grown are distributed to a variety of feeding programs. This abundant harvest is now shared with other urban Episcopal food pantries and a market-style food pantry closer to the neighborhood that is open every day and allows clients to choose their own groceries. Good Shepherd donates food to them at least once a week during the growing season and has developed a good relationship with the staff.

The Peace Meal Project is located at St. John's Episcopal Church in the Tower Grove area of St. Louis. An ecumenical effort with many churches in the area providing food and taking turns preparing a meal, every Saturday night a free dinner is offered to anyone who shows up, no questions asked. A United Thank Offering (UTO) grant in 2007 enabled them to upgrade the church's kitchen to serve these weekly hot meals.

Pamela Dolan,[1] rector and "chief instigator," shares:

Everyone who works in the Shepherd Farm has a different view of this ministry. Some are especially proud of the quantity of food they produce. Others revel in the sense of community and the amazing quality of relationships among the people who garden together. In terms of the plants themselves, many would claim they have best tomatoes in the county. They had so many tomatoes in the first year that they didn't know what to do with them all. The second year they planted far fewer, but the "volunteers" that were created from the seeds of the previous year's fruit, much of which had ended up on the ground before they had a chance to harvest, had other ideas. The people who receive our food always comment on how much flavor it has compared to what they usually eat—an ego boost for any church gardener.

The farmers and gardeners at the Shepherd Farm glory in the ordinary. There is a palpable feeling of awe when working together in the garden, especially at the height of the growing season. It is about much more than the number of pounds harvested or how many families we help feed. The garden is scaled in such a way that we seem to be able to care about every single plant. That sounds sentimental—obviously they have plants that die or are thinned out or never amount to much, just like any garden does. It is less about sentiment and more about lived theology.

Every single plant is a miracle. Every single plant exists only through the grace of God. We don't take any of it for granted.[2]

---

1. Pamela Dolan, "Nearer God's Heart: Church Gardening as a Christian Practice" (DMin thesis, The School of Theology, University of the South, Sewanee, Tennessee, April 2016).

2. Pamela Dolan, e-mail correspondence with author, May 16, 2016.

Plainsong Farm Agricultural evangelist and Episcopal priest Nurya Love Parish has described herself as being called to be a pastor, not a farmer. However, as founder of "The Christian Food Movement," she continues to wonder how we can reimagine food systems in a way that clearly reflects God's reign. Living with her family on a working farm in Rockford, Michigan, she is living out that mission today. In 2016, Plainsong Farm, now partnered with a bonafide farmer, saw its first harvest for Community Supported Agriculture (CSA) with a mission "to practice our faith in place as disciples of Jesus Christ, providing food, hospitality, and farm-based education to those of every faith and none, for the glory of God and the stewardship of God's creation."[3]

---

3. *http://plainsongfarm.com/mission-values/.*

"Consecrating a Garden" at the Trotter Bowl at Virginia Theological Seminary, Alexandria, Virginia (*Photo by Kristin Pitts, courtesy of Robin Denney. Used with permission.*)

Gardens, Workers, and Bees

Cultivate VTS, Virginia Theological Seminary, Alexandria, Virginia

What began as a few small vegetable plots in the front yard of one professor's home has turned into an expansive sustainable gardening model and started conversations about sustainability and theology of the future on a seminary campus. Students interested in sustainable farming and gardening began in earnest to make this a reality by starting the Trotter Bowl (named after a former dean) prayer garden, an herb garden near the seminary's refectory, and a wheat plot during the 2013–2014 term.

By the next academic year, the gardens increased to six, beekeeping was added, and the wheat plot was moved and enlarged. As the seminary engaged in a strategic plan for the future, the gardens became part of the vision. The gardens have become a teaching and learning experience for seminarians, as well as a place for community engagement. The varieties of gardens cultivated are also meant to be models that can be replicated in different kinds of environments that seminarians might encounter in parish ministry in the future. They are also meant to spark people's imagination to think outside the raised-bed gardening model. While raised beds are good, they take a lot of space, work, and resources to install. By providing a number of models (urban, wheat, kitchen, herb, straw bale, vineyard, bees, and compost operation), every parish (with their newly ordained clergy or lay leader) may find a model that could work for their context and locale.

The Trotter Bowl garden is laid out in concentric circles, reminiscent of a labyrinth. It is a functional and prayerful space for growing flowers and vegetables. The wheat garden grows both wheat and rice for flour for communion bread. The field is laid out with a cross-shaped path. Each quadrant uses a different planting technique for wheat (the rice was added later when the wheat flooded). Two varieties of upland rice (not flooded) were transplanted in May 2016, with a plan to harvest in August.

The gardens also provide a means of theological education. A popular event included learning how to prune and graft grapevines, along with a New Testament professor talking about vine metaphors in the Bible. Seminarians especially seem eager to learn about the agriculture metaphors in Scripture for sermon fodder!

Bees! In 2015 Jenifer Gamber (class of 2018) brought beekeeping to Cultivate VTS with two hives for an apiary of garden pollinators. While one hive did not survive the winter, the remaining hive grew so quickly the colony was divided into two. Half the bees were given a new home with a new locally reared queen. The apiary continued to expand when student beekeepers captured a local swarm that had taken up temporary residence in a shrub next to the VTS Welcome Center. By fall 2016, the apiary produced seventy pounds of honey that was distributed to the over two hundred–member VTS community. Plans are in the works to expand the apiary and involve beekeepers of all ages.

The different gardens simulate different challenges, models, or environments where parish gardening might be happening, serving as a model for seminarian learning. Each year, new students arrive on campus, many interested in sustainable farming and gardening, thus ensuring a flow of new ideas and volunteers. While many may not have previous experience, they are willing to help and learn to keep the gardens alive and thriving. Tours are regularly given to visitors on campus, which invigorates everyone.

Take an auditory tour of all the **VTS gardens**. *www.missionalvoices.com /cultivate-vts-garden-tour/.*

Robin Denney (class of 2017) shares:

As much as possible, many reclaimed materials from campus (compost, leaf mulch, wood chips, cardboard, wood, windows, bricks, and so on) are used, always trying to model sustainable practices. Methods that can be used by subsistence farmers are preferred, both because some of our students are from places or will be going to places where they will be working with subsistence farmers, but also as an act of solidarity with those who farm as a means to survival. Some of these techniques, which increase yield in small-scale farming, are also an increase in labor. This labor connects us with the real cost of food production, and gives us an appreciation both for small scale farmers and for the food we eat.[1]

In many ways, the gardens at Virginia Seminary are unlike most gardens. The produce goes to the volunteers, the campus refectory, and the local food bank. The focus of their efforts is not on the produce, but on the process, the learning, and the engagement. Cultivate VTS is a joint effort between students, staff, and faculty. There are relationships (not formal partnerships) with local master gardeners, a food bank, adjacent Episcopal High School, and St. Stephen's and St. Agnes School. Funding is primarily through the VTS sustainability budget, a community engagement fellowship (Seminaries that Change the World), and a UTO seminarian grant.

Bordering Virginia Seminary is **Episcopal High School** with its own 120 acres and a number of gardening and environmental stewardship initiatives. Their student-led sustainable organic garden provides food for the hungry in Arlington. Most of the produce has gone to the Plant a Row for the Hungry Campaign.[2]

As with all gardens, there are challenges. And Cultivate VTS has experienced them all, which have been incorporated into their learning and modification. There was a crop failure (wheat) one year due to pests, birds, and flooding, which led to moving the garden. Mildew and pests, an "Armageddon"

---

1. Robin Denney, conversation with author at Virginia Theological Seminary, October 27, 2016.

2. *www.episcopalhighschool.org/student_life/environmental-sustainability/index.aspx* and *www.foodgatherers.org/*.

of weeds, and hungry deer has led to crop rotation, fencing, and more use of cardboard and woodchips. Motivating and maintaining a consistent volunteer base has been difficult as the times when a lot of labor is needed occur regardless of the semester schedule of classes, studying, and exams.

In addition to the chapel, library, refectory, administration buildings, and student housing VTS houses on its eighty-eight acres, it hosts a diversity of agricultural initiatives. While preparing future leaders for the Church, God's creation is celebrated and visible to all who visit both EHS and VTS campuses. Perhaps as these seminarians are planted in new congregations, they will begin tilling the soil as well as opening up God's message to others in their future ministry and to future generations.

"The Nursery Play Garden" at St. John's in the Wilderness in Denver (*Photo by Kris Stoever. Used with permission.*)

The Cathedral Learning Garden
St. John's in the Wilderness, Denver, Colorado

I t began with a children's garden. Secured by lock and key behind a ten-foot ornamental fence that met historic landmark standards, the nursery garden was redone during the cathedral's 150th anniversary, also marking the 100th anniversary of the cathedral building, completed in 1911. The space would become less formal, a real place for children. The new garden would incorporate flowers for pollinators and herbs for children to care for and learn from. It would be a sensory delight: a play garden.

During the summer of 2010, gardening was a focus of the children's summer camp. One volunteer taught the children how to compost. Indoors there was a worm farm, supplied with scraps by the Sunday school children. Outside the basil plants grew and grew, besieged with honeybees. But come September, two women, new to the cathedral community, stood outside the garden and realized that no one had harvested the basil.

According to Kris Stoever, lead gardener at St. John's,

The garden ministry at Saint John's was born at that moment, when the two women mustered enough indignation to *do something*. They would harvest the basil. The following spring they further resolved that they would not only plant, but this time tend the garden. And they would do it again the spring after that, and so on.

Six years later, in 2016, the garden has been planted anew, and about seven other volunteers have joined the two women. The ministry raises awareness in the congregation about hunger, was declared a Jubilee Parish Ministry in 2015, and has grown, gleaned, and delivered about ten thousand pounds of just-harvested produce toward hunger relief.[1]

Saint John's Cathedral sits atop a hill overlooking the city of Denver. A gothic cathedral made of limestone with a nave 65 feet high, 185 feet long, and 52 feet wide, it stands out in its urban neighborhood. Blessed with an abundance of resources (land, sunshine, soil, water, people, money, relationships), Saint John's has been able to grow food for the hungry and to grow awareness about hunger in Colorado, an agricultural state.

Funding has come from a variety of areas and there are numerous partnerships within the Denver community. In the beginning (2010), funding was received from the cathedral's anniversary committees and the "Green Team," who provided generous in-kind donations. In subsequent years, grants have been obtained from a local group to cover seedlings, and a Mother's Day Plant & Flower Market sells vegetable and herb seedlings. Nursery stock is sent home with gardener volunteers, as gifts, and planted in the raised beds of the play garden and in the landscape generally. Roses and clematis coexist with tomatoes and peppers, engaging volunteers who are food gardeners as well as those who enjoy tending flower gardens.

The Cathedral Bees were installed on the roof of Saint John's, overlooking All Souls' Walk, the summer of 2014 by Charles LaFond, the canon steward, a beekeeper from New Hampshire. The bees were maintained at first by cathedral staff, then by trained beekeepers from the community. There is now a professional apiarist in charge. In return for space on the grounds of the cathedral for his hives, he has offered to care for the cathedral bees on a pro bono basis. This is a popular volunteer ministry at Saint John's.

The Cathedral Co-operative of Gardeners (CCG) plant, tend, glean, and deliver nutritious and freshly harvested produce throughout the growing season. On Sundays, the CCG collects parishioner-grown produce for Monday delivery to Metro Caring, a hunger-relief agency a few blocks away.

---

1. Kris Stoever, e-mail correspondence with author, September 2, 2016.

As with other church-based garden ministries, volunteers are the most challenging piece. For Saint John's, finding volunteers to deliver produce to Metro Caring and scheduling waterers to water can be a struggle. As Kris shares, "In short, growing more than a hundred pounds of food a year in the space is hard. In July, the cruelest month, volunteer gardeners are scarce just as the watering needs are most intense." The cathedral does not have a groundskeeper, so adult gardeners need to make sure the bindweed, mallow, chamomile, and ivy don't overtake the gravel paths. However, they have noticed that children playing can be a weed suppressant!

Partners include many civic organizations: Grow Local Colorado, a coalition of gardeners that grows food in civic parks and other public spaces, including the Governor's Mansion, has been an early encourager; Slow Food, Denver, which began the Seed to Table movement in the Denver Public Schools, where children are taught to grow food in their school gardens for their school cafeterias; Plant a Row for the Hungry (Colorado), an arm of the Association for Garden Communicators; Denver Urban Gardens, an organization that builds and supports urban community gardens in Denver; and Denver Food Rescue, a bicycle-powered food-reclamation group. Partnerships are ecumenical also: the Colorado Council of Churches; Wartburg West, part of Wartburg College in Waverly, Iowa, which is a Lutheran urban internship program headquartered at Saint John's; and Metro Caring, a hunger-relief agency that provides supportive services.

Saint John's has been surprised that by hosting a CSA (Community-Supported Agriculture), they have become the most productive faith community in town. Each year unclaimed shares, left by busy or forgetful CSA members, pay forward more than two thousand pounds of locally grown food to hungry people. All that is required is a shaded corner of a parking lot (or a classroom inside) and a volunteer coordinator. Being a host site declares solidarity with local farmers (and their families) and announces the church's values to their neighborhoods. Hosting a CSA supports local farming families financially and it supports health and wellness in the parish and beyond.

Kris explained how the CSA works at Saint John's:

> At Saint John's we have Wednesday CSA distribution, and it brings crates (called shares) of fresh food for the two-dozen-plus members, or shareholders. Thursday

mornings during the CSA season, one volunteer can expect to deliver entire shares not claimed the previous evening. On the rare Thursday all shares have been claimed, we stack crates and tidy up and declare victory. On other Thursdays ten crates stuffed with fresh produce remain unclaimed—easily two hundred pounds of food at weigh-in. We call this ministry "gleaning."

Over the twenty-six-week growing season more than two thousand pounds of unclaimed food—locally and organically grown produce (vegetables, herbs, and fruit), plus grass-finished meats, local cheese, mushrooms, pastured eggs, and Colorado's famed Noosa yogurt—are taken to our community partner in hunger relief for distribution. They provide supportive social services too, so people can find jobs or job training.[2]

What began as a vision to open up the Nursery Play Garden, the site of the first food garden at Saint John's, has become a hunger-relief ministry. Gardens can now be found on the east and west sides of the cathedral. The future will see a new opportunity soon to grow on the sunbaked south lawn—a 17-bed learning garden, funded with a $30K grant from the Mayor's Office of Economic Development. Partnerships continue, and God's gardens continue to grow physically and spiritually.

---

2. Kris Stoever, e-mail correspondence with author, September 2, 2016.

"Native Corn" at Good Shepherd Mission in Fort Defiance, Arizona (*Photo by Cynthia Hizer. Used with permission.*)

7

Blue Corn and More

Navajoland in Arizona, New Mexico, and Utah

Navajoland Area Mission is comprised of a number of Episcopal missions in New Mexico, Arizona, and Utah that serve 250,000 people on the Navajo reservation. Covering 27,000 square miles and once part of three dioceses (Arizona, Rio Grande, and Utah) that were located within the Navajo Nation, Navajoland now functions much like its own diocese, but with more oversight from the Office of the Presiding Bishop and the House of Bishops. Bishop David Bailey is helping the many mission churches find ways to become sustainable, and gardening has become a large piece of making that a reality. Growing produce for family food as well as marketable goods go hand-in-hand with helping teach new skills to the next generation.

Approximately 43 percent of the Navajo people live below the poverty level, with many children left on the reservation under the care of their grandparents while their parents leave for extended periods of time to work. The Episcopal missions continue to seek ways to bring economic sustainability to its people as well as retaining traditions to pass along to the next generation. Sustainable farming, aquaponics, beekeeping, soap[1] and tea production are just a few of the projects underway across the dry, high desert.

Good Shepherd Mission in Fort Defiance, Arizona, was founded as a medical mission in 1894. Today it has an organic/permaculture garden that uses ancient Navajo gardening techniques alongside modern methods of harvesting water to

---

1 SHIMA´ of Navajoland is a 501(c)(3) nonprofit organization that creates and sells products made from the land such as handmade soap created from herbs, flowers, berries, saps, and oils. *https://shima-of-navajoland.myshopify.com.*

combat the dryness of the climate, allowing crops to grow. For this they received a United Thank Offering Grant (named "Protecting the Precious") of $41,500. Cynthia Hizer, Good Shepherd's vicar, uses a garden plot technique called "cross hatching." Dirt is built up like a giant waffle so that water can collect at the bottom of each square and doesn't run off.[2] Blue corn is also grown, shucked, and dried so it can be turned into flour.

In Bluff, Utah, Leon Sampson began Homer Dale Community Farm on the grounds of St. Christopher's Mission. He initially began it as a family plot for his wife and three children and realized how difficult it was to maintain a plot that had once been fertile for farming and grazing, but had become less so due to environmental degradation. Watching his children learn how to work hard and be overjoyed to eat what they had grown, he knew that his community could experience the same sense of accomplishment and joy. The second season his plot grew and became the Community Farm. He took on the role of farm manager and assisted others in starting their own plots of corn, squash, and melons. There are currently five rows of plots, 10 feet wide by 60 feet long; each family can choose how much they want to call their own. He hopes they will become a business farm, following the model that Thistle Farms[3] has made so successful in Nashville.

First Nations' Kitchen is a ministry of All Saints' Episcopal Indian Mission in Minneapolis and has been serving healthy, organic, traditional indigenous food in a welcoming family environment every Sunday evening since November 2, 2008. Under the leadership of the Reverend Canon Robert Two Bulls, all are welcome at the table. First Nations' Kitchen serves primarily indigenous people in the Twin Cities, particularly residents of nearby Little Earth of the United Tribes, the largest indigenous urban housing community in the United States. First Nations' Kitchen models environmentally sustainable practices in all aspects of the program (composting, recycling) and serves fare based on

Continued

2. *http://episcopaldigitalnetwork.com/ens/2016/09/30/navajo-mission-finds-fertile-ground-for-water-preservation-project/* (accessed October 28, 2016).

3. *http://thistlefarms.org.*

Continued
an ancestral diet of First Nations people (buffalo, wild rice, elk, fish, deer, and turkey). Through a grant from the United Thank Offering, they were able to put in a traditional Three Sisters Garden[4] of corn, squash, and beans. According to native tradition, these three vegetables are inseparable sisters who only grow and thrive together. Every week, First Nations' Kitchen also rescues (or receives donations of unused food from local restaurants) and distributes fresh, organic produce both to dinner guests and to underserved people throughout Minneapolis and St. Paul.

Funding comes from a variety of sources. By collecting cans along the roadside, members redeem them for cash that provides gas for the tractor. A UTO grant was provided to Good Shepherd Mission and St. Christopher's Mission for a seed hopper and equipment to dehydrate, grind, and process the blue corn that is harvested. Growing blue corn is a collaborative business model that will provide income from the selling of blue corn flour (with recipes on the back of the bags). In the future there will be a blue corn fry bread mix, blue corn muffin mix, and the list could go on. A collaborative grant was also received for bees. There are currently fourteen hives in three regions in Navajoland. This sustainable honey crop will be used for making soap.

Leon, a trained chef, now a deacon and attending Virginia Theological Seminary, explained how the Community Farm has become a community enterprise:

We are motivated. Our bishop [David Bailey] supports us in our efforts to create income so that we can become sustainable. Every one of our projects is developed so our community members can learn and become confident entrepreneurs. Digging and discovering fresh spring water is important for three to four families to share with one another. Providing community plots with wide rows allow those who are disabled and in wheelchairs to tend their own gardens. We want to engage the grandparents in teaching the younger generations how to grow food. Navajo kids are isolated; by teaching them new skills we can keep them out of gangs and away from spending all their time on TV or video games. They need more

---

4. www.aihd.ku.edu/gardens/ThreeSistersGarden.html.

challenges, and we try to provide them: academic assistance, life skills such as cooking healthy food that we grow, and developing a good work ethic. Encouraging the grandparents to teach them how to plant corn, squash, and melons also gives room for the sharing of stories, spirituality, and prayer.

There is a story of a young man with a mother and grandmother. They wanted a garden, so I got the ground ready for them and irrigated it. I showed the young man where to plant the seeds and told him that as we push each seed into the soil, we put good thoughts into the ground. He then took the pack of seeds and began to slowly poke holes in the soil and plant each seed. As he did so, he softly spoke. His grandmother noticed, "This is the first time he is praying." I came back later in the season, and this plot had the tallest corn. It's learning how to be humble. That's what it's all about. Creating space to allow it to happen."[5]

Asset Base Community Development (ABCD) has also become involved in supporting the Homer Dale Community Garden. In 2014, the Aneth Community Court Pilot Project began having their clients work the farm by plowing, planting, setting water pipes, irrigation, and hoeing on a weekly basis. Besides fulfilling their community service, they have gained a sense of accomplishment by learning new skills and seeing the fruits of their labors.

Before Leon headed off to seminary, he plowed the fields for families. He looks forward to teaching the next generation (his thirteen-year-old nephew) how to drive the tractor. And his sixteen-year-old son is learning from a local bee advocate how to be a beekeeper. Agricultural initiatives help create memories and sustainability for the future.

---

5. Leon Sampson, interview with author, October 15, 2016 at Virginia Theological Seminary, Alexandria, Virginia.

"Planting in the City" at St. Paul and the Redeemer in Chicago (*Photo by George Chlipala. Used with permission.*)

8

The SPR Food Garden
St. Paul and the Redeemer, Chicago, Illinois

"Let's plant a parable!" Inspired by the parable of the mustard seed, Jim Schall uses that motto to explain the teaching mission of the SPR Food Garden. Starting in 2012 with the Abundant Life Garden Project curriculum developed by Episcopal Relief & Development, the SPR Food Garden has become an integral part of the church's one-week vacation Bible camp. Each day of camp, more than sixty neighborhood kids learn about food and faith through half-hour garden sessions tied in with Godly Play stories, music, crafts, and games—and then they enjoy the fruits of the garden at snack time!

> **The Abundant Life Garden Project** is an interactive, Scripture-based children's program offered to parishes, teachers, families, and others who seek to share the ministry and work of Episcopal Relief & Development with elementary school–aged children. Free and downloadable, it invites children to participate in Episcopal Relief & Development's mission by exploring five thematic lessons on water, seeds, soil, animals, and harvest.[1]

Located in one of Chicago's worst food deserts, the SPR Food Garden grows wholesome vegetables, fruits, and herbs and gives them to people who all too often must subsist on canned, boxed, and junk food. Now having completed its fourth growing season, over 4,000 pounds of nutritious and delicious

---

1. See *http://www.episcopalrelief.org/church-in-action/christian-formation/christian-formation-for-children#Abundant.*

food has been delivered to local soup kitchens, shelters, and food pantries; the annual harvest averages 1,200 pounds per year. The mission of the SPR Food Garden, as Jim Schaal, former garden coordinator, describes it, is fourfold: "To grow food, to serve neighbors, to cultivate community, and to care for creation."[2]

Located on the border between the Hyde Park and Kenwood neighborhoods on the South Side of Chicago, St. Paul and the Redeemer Episcopal Church's garden is situated in front of the church on a busy residential street. Just south of the garden is the front entrance of the church, which also serves as portal to their SPR Food Pantry. With no fence, it is freely open to visitors.

The garden helps to connect the parish to the neighborhood in several ways. The openness and attractiveness of the garden often draws interest from passersby. As a place of service and learning, the garden connects volunteer groups from nearby schools, seminaries, and the university. As a public symbol of community engagement, the garden bears witness to the parish's core value of radical hospitality. Several groups are welcomed each year for tours and service learning events, including groups from the Chicago Master Gardeners, the University of Chicago Divinity School, the Lutheran School of Theology at Chicago, and a nearby Montessori school.

It all began with a partnership with KAM Isaiah Israel Congregation, a nearby Reform synagogue in 2012. They had started a food garden beginning in 2009, and with encouragement of the rector (Peter Lane), a parishioner (Jim Schaal) worked with members of KAMII to develop the concept for a new garden and construction plan. Jim followed up with a proposal to the vestry, which voted unanimously in support of it; two weeks later, sod was being dug up to build the new garden. The active involvement of clergy and vestry has been a key to the garden's success.

Jim describes the garden:

> The SPR Food Garden includes plantings of native prairie wildflowers and edible annual flowers to attract bees, butterflies, birds, and other pollinators. A small bed of fragrant culinary herbs welcomes visitors at each entrance to the garden, and we invite our neighbors to help themselves to herbs throughout the week.

---

2. Jim Schaal, e-mail correspondence with author, August 15, 2016.

Behind our small garden shed we compost our garden and landscape waste in large bins, producing about two cubic yards of finished compost each year through aerobic hot composting followed by slow vermicomposting.[3]

Using sustainable practices of crop rotation and succession planting, the crop list and planting plan adapts to meet the changing needs of the food recipients each season. Each year a few new crops are added as an experiment, and in 2017 there are hopes to expand the garden beds.

The weekend harvest is presented along with monetary offerings and food pantry donations at the Sunday Eucharist. Today, most of the harvest goes to St. Martin de Porres House of Hope, a women and children's shelter in the nearby Woodlawn neighborhood. The shelter shares any excess harvest with a public housing project for seniors across the street. Beginning in 2016, a portion of the harvest is being distributed through SPR's recently expanded Food Pantry, now serving thirty-five to fifty households per week.

The SPR Food Garden cultivates community in ways both highly intentional and delightfully unexpected. The regular gardeners, a core group of about twelve parishioners and community members, all unpaid volunteers, have grown to know and care deeply for one another through shared labors and deep conversations. About six to eight volunteers participate each week in a two-hour Saturday morning garden session. Four of the volunteers, including the Food Garden coordinator, are experienced enough to lead garden sessions. The Food Garden coordinator commits an additional four to six hours per week to planning tasks, coordinating volunteers, purchasing materials, and other responsibilities. Occasional volunteers are greeted warmly too, and a special effort is made to welcome children to participate.

Jim describes how the garden has also become a center of worship:

The SPR Food Garden was designed from the beginning as a liturgical space, laid out along the lines of a traditional church nave. A historic stone baptismal font, a silent witness to the catastrophic fire that destroyed our previous church building in 1958, stands at the south entrance. A handsome cedar communion table, custom built by the carpenter who built our columbarium, awaits at the north

---

3. Jim Schaal, e-mail correspondence with author, August 15, 2016.

end—and behind it stands a reredos of prairie coneflowers and culinary herbs. In between are aisles, lined with locally sourced woodchips, where the assembly can gather. In fitting sacramental fashion, each also has a common use: the table as workbench, the font as birdbath, and the aisles as wheelbarrow paths.

In this space we have celebrated the dedication of the garden on Earth Sunday 2012, rogation days in the springtime, and harvest blessings in the autumn. From Palm Sunday processionals to Maundy Thursday prayers, the garden is a stage for Holy Week; during the Easter Sunday egg hunt and the St. Francis Pet Blessing, it is an arena for playful days. Each Sunday during the growing season, we bring the harvest into the main sanctuary and place it around the table at the Eucharist—and sometimes it is brought in with the offerings by a procession of children and parents.[4]

The SPR Food Garden is just one of several ways the parish seeks to serve its neighbors both locally and globally. In addition to the Food Pantry, the Open Kitchen prepares monthly meals to be served to about two hundred homeless neighbors at a nearby interfaith soup kitchen. Friends of Shoesmith (a public elementary school across the street) have recently fostered a partnership with another nonprofit gardening and nutrition education program. Partnerships with two parishes in Haiti have promoted fair trade, fostered community economic development, and provided disaster relief; currently the parish sponsors a free lunch program for some 175 students there. As each of these outreach ministries has grown, food and feeding has become a unifying theme of the parish's public engagement.

Theologically speaking, Jim calls this "ministry of feeding the hungry a richly embodied, almost sacramental expression of the radical hospitality to which we are called by Jesus Christ and to which we are moved by the Holy Spirit in response to God's grace."[5] The memorial bench in the SPR Food Garden bears an inscription quoting Fred Clark, the late father of parishioner Allison Clark. His bequest now supports the garden: "Because planting a garden is an act of faith."

---

4. Jim Schaal, e-mail correspondence with author, August 15, 2016.
5. Ibid.

Truman Heminway became a farmer-priest at Church of Our Saviour in Sherburne, Vermont, in 1931, following in the footsteps of several priests. The farm was established and settled in the early nineteenth century by Josiah Wood, a veteran of the Revolutionary War and War of 1812, in the Sherburne Valley, later to be given to the Diocese of Vermont to support a priest in the area in the 1890s. The Heminways worked the Mission Farm even though they were not native-bred farmers and needed to learn new skills. He got up before the sun to do the early chores, recite Morning Prayer, and perform his other devotions. After a hearty break-fast, Truman and his wife remained at table (often with guests) to read aloud from a book, often theological. Then it was "off to the work of the farm: animals to tend, barns to clean, wood to cut, fields to plow, plant, and harvest, machinery to repair, gates and fences to mend." In the eve-ning, he would put on his cassock (over his corduroy trousers and blue working shirt) to toll the bell for Evensong for the neighboring farmers. Dinner followed back at the house, often with the worshippers joining them. On Sunday morning at nine o'clock Morning Prayer was said, fol-lowed by the Choral Eucharist. For more than a quarter of a century, the Heminways provided spiritual care as well as conversation to the farm-ing community. In 1957, Father Heminway donned his cassock for the last time, approached the altar to begin the service, collapsed, and qui-etly breathed his last.[6]

---

6. These stories were discovered in a booklet written by H. Boone Porter Jr. entitled, *Truman Heminway: Priest-Farmer,* published by the National Council in New York for 25¢ in 1961 and held in a collection at the Library of the School of Theology at the University of the South, Sewanee, Tennessee.

"The Gospel Garden" at St. Mark's, New Canaan, Connecticut (*Photo by Sharon Ely Pearson. Used with permission.*)

Community Gardens
Ministry Network
The Episcopal Church in Connecticut

Traffic was backed up and it would take almost two hours, but the gardeners from St. John's in Vernon, St. Andrew's in Madison, and Church of the Holy Advent in Clinton were determined to see the Gospel Garden at St. Mark's in New Canaan at the other end of I-95 in Connecticut. They were just a few of the ten to fifteen churches that participate in the Episcopal Church in Connecticut's (ECCT) Community Gardens Ministry Network. The purpose of the network is to see each other's garden space, share stories and experiences regarding the season's gardens, and gain support from one another by sharing best practices—along with the joys, frustrations, and enthusiasm for engaging in agriculture ministry.

Their most recent gathering took place on a blustery fall day in the waning sunlight.[1] Bishop Suffragan Laura Ahrens momentarily took a seat on the "sod chair," laughingly calling it her cathedra. The Gospel Garden at St. Mark's has a new director, Margaret Roscoe, who proudly shared the various areas of the garden with the visitors. She admits to being a novice and dependent on her predecessor Brian Hollstein, a 2010 Connecticut Master Gardener graduate. Established about ten years ago on top of an unused swimming pool and tennis court, the garden of raised boxes produced almost two thousand pounds of lettuces, asparagus, chard, broccoli, tomatoes, cucumbers, eggplants, beets,

---

1. All quotes in this chapter are from this network's gathering on October 23, 2016, at St. Mark's Episcopal Church, New Canaan, Connecticut.

beans, celery, potatoes, kale, herbs, and more in 2016. All fresh produce is given to the New Canaan Food Pantry that feeds close to two hundred people every two weeks. Flowers grown are shared with members of the parish as well as a local nursing home, food pantry clients, and the church's side chapel. Volunteers from the Boy and Girl Scouts, National Charity League, SLOBS (Service League of Boys), New Canaan Beautification League, and other local groups have built walkways, composting bins, a storage shed, a turf sofa, a picnic table, a sundial, birdhouses, and have contributed an endless list of improvements and enhancements.

After exploring the Gospel Garden, the gardeners moved indoors to share stories. Margaret spoke about the volunteers who have worked the garden at St. Mark's. She spoke of the nineteen-year-old volunteer who loved to come and harvest, but was especially happy as she delivered the food to the pantry; the day school preschoolers who help plant seeds in the spring; the local nursery that donated plants; and the mentally challenged adults who come to visit and help with simple tasks.

Margaret Larom, director of the Food for All Garden in Clinton, notes that their garden is located behind the church (Holy Advent) but between an elementary school and a residential Alzheimer's care facility. Children come to explore the garden, teenagers come to do community service, and those with wheelchairs, walkers, and dementia come accompanied by their aides to sort cherry tomatoes into baskets, put herbs in baggies, or watch others at work.

Peter Larom, vicar of Holy Advent, calls the ministry of church agriculture and gardening as providing a "missionary destination." "Where else do people from all walks of life, all ages, all abilities, and all persuasions come out of curiosity and hunger for the spiritual as well as the physical? In a garden you have relationships with folks you would never otherwise run into."

Many of the church gardens in this ECCT network contribute to the Shoreline Soup Kitchens & Pantries, an interfaith service that provides food and fellowship to those in need and educates the community on hunger and poverty. It serves people who live in eleven communities near the Connecticut River and Long Island Sound. In addition to meals, fresh produce is offered at various locations on different days of the week.

One of the participants in the Shoreline Soup Kitchens & Pantries is the Common Good Gardens in Old Saybrook. The idea for the garden came in 2002 when Claudia Van Ness, then a reporter for the *Hartford Courant*, interviewed the then-new director of the Shoreline Soup Kitchen & Pantries and learned that they needed fresh vegetables. Claudia was also the president of a local garden club at the time, so she invited all the area garden clubs' members to come together to figure out how they could grow produce together for the pantries. Grace Episcopal Church (which is one of the pantry sites) donated a large piece of land behind the church (at first 1/5 of an acre; today it spans ¾ of an acre). Claudia shares, "It's important to note that none of this would be possible without the stalwart support of Grace Church, which supplies our water, land, meeting space and so much more."

Food Pantries Once an emergency stopgap for families in a difficult situation—for example, where income earners have lost their jobs—food pantries in lower Fairfield County, Connecticut (with some of the wealthiest towns in the United States) increasingly have become a more regular source of sustenance on which many families have come to rely. Another example is St. Gregory of Nyssa in San Francisco. They have a food pantry like few others. Every Friday, around the same altar where St. Gregory's offers communion, free groceries are given away to four hundred hungry families, providing literally tons of fresh fruits and vegetables, rice, beans, pasta, cereal, and bread.[2]

Common Goods is now a 501(C)(3) nonprofit corporation tended by a large cadre of volunteers—thirty who are regulars—who grow and deliver the produce to the five Shoreline Soup Kitchen pantries each week. Rows and rows of fruits and vegetables grow from early spring through fall, including blueberry bushes (covered with net canopies to keep out the wildlife), squash, asparagus, varieties of eggplant, tomatoes, cabbage, green peppers, and more. In addition, volunteers pick up day-old vegetables and fruit from six farm stands and also deliver that produce to the pantries. About eight thousand pounds of vegetables

---

2. The beginnings of this ministry are shared in Sara Miles' book *Take This Bread: A Radical Conversion* (New York: Ballantine Books, 2008).

were grown in the 2016 season. From Common Good Gardens' Facebook page on July 14, 2016:

> Today we harvested 210 pounds of herbicide- and pesticide-free vegetables; Tuesday it was 290 pounds. It is all delivered to the food pantries in Old Saybrook, Westbrook, Old Lyme, and Niantic within hours of being picked.[3]

This organic garden is tended by the community from far and wide, each offering their own skills and time, making this a venture based on cooperation, shared vision, and responsibility. Some garden club members still participate; other volunteers arrive through word of mouth, ads in the local papers, the master gardening program, and even the courts. Teens are considered a highly valuable asset for their energy and strength. Claudia explains two elements that make them unique:

> Our garden is organic and we grow everything in the compost we make in twenty-four bins. With research and experimentation, we can make compost in six weeks, instead of the usual year or so. We've introduced a number of other innovations to our operation to make it as efficient and high yielding as possible. Local coffee shops even donate their coffee grounds.
>
> A team of sailors from the nearby Groton naval submarine base prepares the garden beds at the beginning and end of the season (twice a year) on "Navy Day." They arrive at 8:00 a.m. and work through the day, shutting down and detaching the various systems, such as the irrigation pipelines, and removing dead roots, overgrowth, and debris from the soil and fencing. It is a day of heavy lifting as well as fellowship as it is "all hands on deck" in the garden to work, with breaks to share breakfast and lunch together.[4]

In Clinton, the Food for All Garden has 75 4-foot wide beds on a 30-foot long plot that produced 9,200 pounds of fresh produce in 2016; four years ago (their first year) they grew 3,750 pounds. Margaret (Larom) admits to not being a "professional" gardener, but she shares her wisdom and experience with the rest of the group: how and where to seek grants; why it's important to

3. www.facebook.com/CommonGoodGardensOS/posts/493705650823983.

4. Claudia Van Ness, e-mail correspondence with author, October 26, 2016.

keep track of volunteers and the hours they give; how to communicate with the parish, volunteers, and community.

But the ECCT garden network is not just about comparing poundage, crops, and volunteers—although those are important topics. It is about sharing ideas and how this ministry is rooted (no pun intended) in God's creation. Virginia Army of St. John's, Vernon, and coordinator of the network, shares how they harvest their garden between their two Sunday morning services, blessing the produce at the second service as the fruit of earth. They raise money for their garden by growing pumpkins, which they "recycle" by selling as pies or for jack o' lanterns. Their organic produce is given to the Cornerstone Food Pantry. She also shares that to the west and across the Connecticut River, St. James', West Hartford, grows herbs that they dry or make into pesto to sell at their holiday fair, with proceeds going toward outreach.

Gary and Brenda Naegel of St. Andrew's, Madison, oversee several plots at Bower Park, a town community garden consisting of 140 plots of 20 feet by 20 feet each on 64 acres. While their garden is not on the church's property, they constructed four small raised beds for herbs and flowers near a church entrance that receives high visibility. While not everyone travels to the garden in Bower Park, parishioners are reminded of the vision in this welcoming spot. The congregation celebrates Rogation Sunday with prayer, readings by the gardeners, and everyone processing to this small garden for a blessing.

Peter Larom adds his view of what community agricultural ministry is all about in addition to it being a ministry to others. Gardens can be a destination for some, and an introduction to a lifestyle to others. He explains it is a three-part ministry:

1. "Dig and Pick": tilling the soil, planting, and harvesting;
2. "Collaboration" of working together, consulting, and sharing wisdom;
3. "Downstream Ministry" in which 90 percent of those who come to the garden may not add money or labor, but it offers them a place of serenity, learning, and peace.

The conversation turns to frustrations: drought, bugs and blights, weeds, and varmints. It also turns humorous: comparing worms and what is caught in catch-and-release traps. Lettie Nagles of St. John's, Vernon:

We had a problem with woodchucks eating everything. We set up some "have a heart" traps to catch and release the culprits. First we caught a skunk. We released her and cleaned out the trap. Then an opossum. We released him and cleaned out the trap. Then a raccoon. We released her, but didn't clean out the trap. The musk he left behind has since kept all the critters away. In addition to the sweat, mulch, and achy muscles, gardening is a messy business.

A network of church gardeners provides support, connection, and laughter. Many who volunteer in these gardens don't belong to the congregations, but working in the garden feels sacred to them. It is a privilege for them, a miracle to be able to plant a seed and watch it grow into a vegetable. Margaret Larom shares:

> [This] is more than a garden. It is a communal experience of working together, sacrificing physical comfort to work. People are surprised to hear how we are totally committed to others—we give everything that is grown away. We don't take any for ourselves. It is like a runaway train, but it is a movement, and I'm excited to be part of it.

"Constructing Raised Beds" at St. Mary Magdalene in Manor, Texas (*Photo courtesy of Alex Montes-Vela. Used with permission.*)

10

Plant a Church: Plant a Garden

St. Mary Magdalene Episcopal Church, Manor, Texas

Manor, Texas, is one of the fastest growing cities in Texas, located twelve miles northeast of Austin. As you drive along Highway 290 between Houston and Texas, you'll see St. Mary Magdalene Episcopal Church (SMM) on a hill, with bright red doors and its cedar walls freshly painted white. The Episcopal Church Welcomes You sign invites passersby to stop in. Located on twenty-three acres, this new congregation is adjusting to a new reality as they begin to create a new history.

In January 2010, Alex Montez-Villa began meeting with a small group of people in the living room of his home. The coffee table was their altar. There were copies of the bilingual Book of Common Prayer on the piano. The Eucharist was celebrated. Later, tortillas were prepared and the grill started for another meal to be shared with this newly planted church community. By late summer 2010, they were worshipping in the cafeteria at Manor High School and still growing. A pattern developed: after worship was concluded and the tables were cleared of liturgical wares, another meal was shared and relationships were strengthened at those same cafeteria tables. Intentionally, all worship and communication is done both in English and Spanish.

The Diocese of Texas purchased the land for Alex and St. Mary Magdalene to build a church. In December 2014, the SMM community moved to its "new" home on the "hill." This first generation bilingual worshipping community that was 99 percent Latino made a leap of faith and are now in their own church building, welcoming families from the greater Manor area to worship and engage with the wider community. Alex shares:

It is like you are living in your car, then suddenly moving to a large house with landscaping and all the amenities. It was a big adjustment. We were a small congregation who knew each other and now we are a diverse congregation where 80 percent of our members have never gone to a church before. We have to adjust to a new reality and create our own history. But we cannot settle down. We need to discern what God has given us; what does God want us to do now? The area of Austin is becoming gentrified and many families are relocating; many who are moving to Manor need support from local agencies. Church planting is about collaboration. And that is what we did.[1]

The congregation and its leadership are participants in Family with Voices/ Familias con Voces Collaborative, a coalition formed to address and support the multiple complex needs of whole families in the Manor Independent School District area. Members of this coalition include Goodwill Industries of Central Texas, Foundation for the Homeless, Easter Seals Central Texas, and Austin Travis County Integral Care. In the spring of 2016, the Foundation for the Homeless team was looking for office space, which St. Mary Magdalene was able to provide for them. It was then that the conversations of creating a community garden at SMM began. Others then stepped in to offer funding.

Alex repeatedly says he has no experience with building a garden. But he has experience with planting. It took a long time driving around Manor in his car before he was able to find a place to locate St. Mary Magdalene's church building. It took the work of digging and discovering the tools that were needed to make it happen. In the hard work, relationships were made stronger and organically things expanded. "Building a church needs to be done in collaboration with others. It cannot be done alone. The stories we tell each other, the jokes, and more . . . these build collective memories."[2] In June 2015 they broke ground for their church building. In August 2016 they broke ground again, going on faith that God would embody the whole community to create a community garden. It too was hard work. The Texas soil is dry, hard clay. When it gets wet it becomes glue-like. But with shovels in hand, Saturday after Saturday, holes were dug for fence posts and as the weeks progressed, raised beds

---

1. Alex Montez-Villa, phone conversation with the author, October 26, 2016.

2. Alex Montes-Villa, phone interview with author, September 26, 2016.

were constructed for all to see. In September, Manor's mayor arrived and cut the ribbon for the garden's official opening.

The garden is still a work in progress. They don't know what the crops will be yet. However, everything harvested will go to food banks and pantries in Manor. Church planters know to let go and allow the community to determine what will be created. Worship will continue, following the pattern that the first church members began: prepare food for each other, eat food with each other, clean up with each other.

Alex says, "We are excited to be working a project that will benefit our surrounding community, and the great opportunity to share our resources." Plans are also underway for offering gardening classes in January 2017, offering tips for individuals and families to take the ideas grown organically (literally and figuratively) at this site to their homes. As St. Mary Magdalene's mission expands, they will continue to keep the real needs of the community in mind. "God has provided. I pray that this will be a picture of what the practice of collaboration with others looks like. It is all about building relationships with our neighbors. Who knows what will be next."

After the 2010 earthquake, the **Diocese of Haiti** and its development arm, Centre Diocesain de Development et de Secours (CEDDISEC), in partnership with Episcopal Relief & Development, launched a program to promote kitchen gardens, which in Creole are called Jardins prè-Kay. CEDDISEC's kitchen garden program seeks to enable families to produce a variety of vegetables and fruit for daily use and sale, improving household food availability and pocket money. Kitchen gardens are versatile in both structure and size, allowing families to create productive gardens inside of old tires, grain sacks, half-barrels, and within very confined spaces. At the same time, by using appropriate techniques, kitchen gardens can grow year-round. CEDDISEC's agriculture objectives are to facilitate people's access to the resources (i.e., techniques, seeds, and tools) necessary to create small kitchen gardens that do not depend upon access to expansive or traditional plots of agricultural land; and to share opportunities for experiential and technical learning that will enable people to engage in vegetable production and diversify vegetable consumption throughout the year without seasonal variations.

"Picking Plums" at Camp Stevens, Julian, California. (*Photo courtesy of Ashley Graham-Wilcox. Used with permission.*)

11

Camps and Conference Centers
Modeling Caring for the Land

The Episcopal Church has over eighty-five camps and conference centers within the United States. From Hawaii's Camp Mokule`ia to Camp Bishopswood in Maine, children, youth, and adults have the opportunity to set a time apart from everyday life, make new friends, and explore God's abundant creation at an Episcopal camp.

Camps have a long history of being connected to tilling the soil. Camp Washington, a camp and conference center of the Episcopal Church in Connecticut, was founded in 1917 by Floyd Steele Kenyon as a summer camp for boys that included growing fields of beans for the war effort. Today raised beds of vegetables can be found alongside some of the buildings. Camp and gardening go hand-in-hand, hoe-to-hoe.

Bill Slocomb, director of Episcopal Camps and Conference Centers, Inc., shares what each have in common:

> Camps and conference centers help the mission of the larger Episcopal Church by providing space for people to connect with God, and space to connect to each other about God. Having meals together, which happens at all camps/centers, is an opportunity and place where these connections can happen. Growing and sharing food as part of the meals adds to the conversation about stewardship of resources and our environmental footprint, while providing healthy, nourishing meals for campers and guests.[1]

---

1. Bill Slocomb, phone conversation with author, September 23, 2016, and e-mail correspondence with author, November 4, 2016.

Agriculture and food ministry has a unique place with camps and centers. For those who live in cities, these places are often the only living example of what it means to eat "farm to table." Meals are a central ministry of camps; it is around the table that we build relationships and learn about what we eat—and don't eat. Learning to put on your plate only what you can eat, and weighing all the excess waste is a learning experience. All ages can be excited (or fearful) of the day's "ort report," the food waste comprised of each person's "morsel left at a meal" on one's plate. Many centers, if they do not have a garden or farm on site, are seeking local partnerships for ordering their fresh produce.

Camps and centers offer educational programs for schools, retreat guests, summer campers, and diocesan ministries year-round. Often, what is learned at these sites is brought back home to implement in a local congregation or community. At the core of most camps is celebrating the gift of God's creation and how we are each called to be better environmental stewards of land, water, and all that grows upon the earth. Camp Stevens in the Diocese of San Diego has a mission focused on environmental sustainability, food justice, and human health concerns. With two gardens and an orchard, plus drought conditions in recent years, their emphasis has been more about education than production. Teaching their camps how to eat healthy and prepare food demystifies the farm to table process. All produce, plus eggs (from forty-five chickens), stays within their programs, going through their kitchen to serve the many visitors, retreat-ants, and campers.

In addition to its organic garden and orchard, **Camp Stevens** raises livestock—chickens and pigs. Shares are sold of the pigs for cash, with the meat processed by another company. The pigs are a great educational tool while also helping with their compost. Beth Bojarski states, "I am proud that this community is united behind our environmental sustainability initiatives, food justice, and food programs that have been put into place here. We care about the health of our pigs. Campers make bread in the kitchen, and press juice from the orchard fruit. They see the flowers and the plums and see how they can be transformed and represent the Body and Blood of Christ from their own hands."[2]

---

2. Beth Bojarski, phone interview with author, November 4, 2016.

There are ten to fifteen camps and centers that have taken a direct lead with having a garden or farm program on site. These include:

- **The Proctor Center** sits on sixty acres of a 1,200+ site in predominately agricultural Madison County, Ohio (Diocese of Southern Ohio). Proctor Farm is a mixed vegetable farm with a mixed fruit tree orchard and a greenhouse for starting seeds. They participate in a local farmers' market May through November and offer CSA shares in addition to contributing to the meals at the Center. Every summer they offer apprenticeships to individuals who desire to gain work experience, teach, and discover new practices on the fully functioning organic farm.

- **Camp Stevens's** organic garden began in 2000 as a small kitchen garden. Today the camp chef can reach out of the back kitchen door to choose from herbs, flowers, and vegetables to bring to table. There is now an orchard with apples, pears, peaches, plums, apricots, cherries, pluots, persimmons, a variety of berries, and much more throughout the seasons. In 2007, on a sunny, south-facing slope north of the camp center a new one-acre terraced garden was begun, called the Phoenix Garden. Here perennials stands of grapes, figs, lavender, and native plants are grown. The integration of chickens and pigs for egg production and culinary use in the kitchen has been added. All serve as an environmental educational piece for guests and campers in the mountains of San Diego.

- **Camp McDowell** is the camp and conference center for the Episcopal Church in Alabama, located in Nauvoo. It includes the McDowell Farm School and the McDowell Environmental Center (*http://mcdowellec.com/*). The Farm School's mission is to inspire curiosity, teach problem solving, and empower community action through sustainable agriculture. Camp McDowell's history is rooted in the land and agriculture. Since its founding in 1947 with summer campers digging potatoes and moving cattle, its programs and initiatives seek to return to managing their own land using sustainable practices, producing food and alternative energy, and creating zero waste. Today they work to put as much local, sustainably grown and healthy food into their dining halls as possible. Since 2014, expansion has included the raising of two barns, a greenhouse, chicken coops and yards, and four acres of crop production.

- **Camp Mokule῾ia** on the north shore of Oahu, Hawaii, focuses on composting and food sustainability projects, a native plant nursery and garden, coastal restoration, and watering.

- **The Rock Point Gardens Project** in Burlington, Vermont, is a collaborative project in the making between the Episcopal Church in Vermont and the surrounding community. The hopes for this unfolding project aims to utilize the land at Rock Point (the largest acreage of open space in Burlington) to teach, innovate, and build community through sustainable food production, ecological design, and environmental education. The vision includes community gardens, a fruit orchard, school gardens (there is a diocesan owned private school on the property), a maple sugaring stand, colonies of bees, and a permaculture project. One of the outcomes of this venture is to generate over three hundred pounds of gleaned food for the Chittenden Emergency Food Shelf.

- **Trinity Retreat Center** was farm and forestland along the Housatonic River, a half-mile east of the village of West Cornwall, Connecticut, a century ago. In the 1930s, the vicar of Trinity Church Wall Street purchased the property so that it could be used as a summer camp for disadvantaged youth from the city. By 1990, the camp had been closed and Trinity decided to expand the main retreat center to turn it into a conference center run by the church, which subsequently closed in 2012. Today Trinity Retreat Center is reimagining how they can reclaim fifty-five acres as farmland where pilgrims from around the world can find God in the soil—whether it's for a month or just a day. Dreams include an orchard in the grassland behind the red barn, which will house goats and chickens; a vegetable farm behind the workshop; hops instead of lawn on the big hill above the main house; hives for honeybees—lots of hives. Hopes of restoring the baseball field on the edge of the forest into a monastic field of dreams where people will gather at the end of the day to play and eat. It will also be a prayerful place, with a full-time priest who will frame much of the programming around the land, stewardship, history, and the next wave of Christianity. Living on monastic time, amid the orchards, the farm, changing river, and fireflies, Trinity will be constantly trying to answer the big questions about the next chapter of the church. The produce will go to the farm-to-table meals, to the staff, to help barter for services locally, to community sharing agreements, to food banks in the region, and to food programs run by Trinity in New York City.

- The gardening program at **Gravatt Farm** at Gravatt Camp and Conference Center in Aiken, South Carolina, began in 2009 with a few small garden boxes and a lot of hope. Of course, that first season ended up producing a basket full of tomatoes—and that was about it. The Gravatt Gardens grew into Camp Gravatt Farms and produced over 4,300 pounds of food in 2014, thanks to a grant from the United Thank Offering, the support of donors, and the dedication of Gravatt staff. Today, guests at the conference center and summer campers enjoy meals prepared with zucchini, squash, okra, tomatoes, greens, cantaloupe, watermelon, and peppers—all picked daily. The kitchen works throughout the year to preserve a great deal of food so guests can enjoy vegetables and soups throughout the year. Gravatt is a Fresh on the Menu member and their produce is Certified SC.[3]

---

3. *www.campgravatt.org/gravattfarms/*.

"Hydroponics at the Cathedral" at the Cathedral of St. Mary in Memphis (*Photo by John Burruss. Used with permission.*)

12

Thistle & Bee

Partnerships in the Diocese of West Tennessee

W hat does a congregation located in the densely populated suburb of Cordova, Tennessee, and one downtown Memphis parish have in common? A partnership. Growing out of the collaboration of clergy and lay leaders of Calvary Episcopal Church in Memphis and Church of the Annunciation in Cordova, Thistle & Bee is now a social enterprise (Friends of Thistle Farms) involving raising bees, growing herbs, and building a business that will help survivors of human trafficking survive.

It began with a simple conversation that grew roots that spread. Eyleen Farmer, associate rector of Calvary, began gathering people in late 2013 to find a way to address the systemic issues of prostitution and sex trafficking in Memphis. Inspiration was provided by Thistle Farms/Magdalene House in Nashville and Becca Stevens, who is a regular preacher at Calvary's annual Lenten preaching series. At the same time, a group of people had begun the Community of St. Therese of Lisieux in midtown Memphis, modeled after Magdalene House in Nashville. Named after St. Theresa of Lisieux, "the Little Flower," they also provide a home for women who have survived trauma, addiction, trafficking, and prostitution.

At a diocesan clergy conference, Farmer shared her passion with then vicar of Church of the Annunciation, John Burruss. While Farmer had been riding in a police cruiser with a local police lieutenant to learn more about the women on the streets in South Memphis, Burruss had been leading Annunciation through a strategic planning process around the stewardship of their twelve acres of land along the Wolf River watershed. Annunciation desired to create a sustainable environment for wildlife on their property, making it open and accessible to the public. They dreamed of birdhouses scattered about, a wild-flower garden for butterflies, and a bee colony on their "sacred grounds."

Thistle Farms is a sanctuary for healing for female survivors of abuse, addiction, trafficking, and prostitution. A community of survivors, advocates, employees, and friends from all across the world that are young and old, women and men, their mission is to change a culture that still allows human beings to be bought and sold. Founder Becca Stevens seeks to share "a farmer's theology" that the world is our farm and we are to cultivate it. This theology is grounded in the idea that love heals and that healing is the most important sacrament of the church. Being a Thistle Farmer means "the world is our field"[1] and that we choose to love all creation.

The sharing of each other's stories at that clergy gathering led to a dialogue between the two congregations. They discovered a shared knowledge of beekeeping. (Calvary parishioners Terri Pervis, Betty Jo Dulaney, and Harriet McFadden, and Annunciation's deacon, David Christian, were all beekeepers.) An interest in developing Annunciation as an apiary emerged; Christian secured two hives in Cookeville, Tennessee, and Calvary purchased the beekeeping equipment and materials. This partnership culminated on May 4, 2014, when members of both congregations gathered to install a small herb garden and have a blessing of the bees. The liturgy ended with Emily Dickinson's Trinitarian blessing, "In the name of the bee, the butterfly, and of the breeze."

Annunciation offered to partner with Calvary to use the land for the development of a farm. Possibly because of the work of the Community of Lisieux, Farmer thought movement toward the creation of a social enterprise first might be the best strategy in Memphis. Could both dreams become a reality through partnership?

---

1. Becca Stevens, *Letters from the Farm: A Simple Path for a Deeper Spiritual Life* (New York: Morehouse Publishing, 2015), 49.

West Tennessee Aquaponics Project A pilot project aimed at raising one hundred pounds of fish and one thousand plants at a time was installed at St. Mary's Episcopal Cathedral in May of 2016. The goal of the project is to employ at least one person from the job-insecure community that worships on Wednesday to care and harvest the food, which will be sold at a farmers' market on a Sunday morning at the church. There even was a "blessing of the catfish and catfish poop." Watch a video of the farmers' market as well as see the aquaponic garden: *https://vimeo.com/189990809*.

Bees solidified the partnership; in September of 2014, thousands of honeybees were found in the historic bell tower of Calvary Church. The bees were extracted and moved to Annunciation, creating the third hive in the apiary. As the project grew, parishioners from both congregations became beekeepers with no prior experience: Mills Polatty, Cary Ciocca, and Drew Lawless. In 2016, Lawless and Polatty are still the primary beekeepers and have developed a love for the craft.

In 2015, Annunciation and Calvary received a UTO grant, which allowed the hiring of a garden and farm manager. In the fall of 2015, they partnered with St. Columba Episcopal Camp and Conference center to build a flower farm and in 2016 established a second apiary. Now twenty hives exist between the two farms. Farmer continued to champion the work of drawing together different voices in the development of what is now Thistle & Bee Enterprises. Farmer describes the business aspect of Thistle & Bee:

> In April of 2016, Thistle and Bee began piloting new products at the Overton Park Farmers' Market. A farmers' market has been the perfect incubator for business ideas and a place to share and talk about the mission of the organization as the Church explores new ways of being involved in the community. The core business has been selling fresh flowers, herb rubs, and fresh squeezed lemonade and ice tea sweetened with the local honey. The business has been selling the drinks by the growler full (64 oz.) where people can get refills each week. The group also began a third garden growing fruits and vegetables near downtown.[2]

---

2. Eyleen Farmer, e-mail correspondence to author, September 2, 2016.

St. Mary's Community Garden was initially funded through a grant from Grow Memphis. It has become a connector between the neighborhood and the cathedral as a ministry of hospitality. Food that is grown is distributed to the local community.

The Community of Lisieux is now a two-year residential program where the women receive healthcare, drug treatment, and counseling. There are hopes that they will be paid to grow herbs and keep bees, as well as process, package, and market what they harvest in the form of consumer goods like herbal tea, honey, and lip balm from the various gardens and hives.

Today, Annunciation's "sacred grounds" offer annual festivals, blessings of animals, picnic areas, and a recreation area for community activities such as volleyball, basketball, softball, and Frisbee. Dogs are also welcome. Local scout troops use the property for campouts and inner city youth enjoy the open space for retreats. Dreams continue for a labyrinth, Stations of the Cross, an outdoor chapel, and more.

It all began with a conversation.

"Bishop Katharine Blessing the New Garden" at St. Augustine of Hippo in Galveston, Texas (*Photo by Richard Schori. Used with permission.*)

13

Plot against Hunger
Church of Our Saviour Farm, Dallas, Texas

O ur Saviour Episcopal Church was founded in 1955 in the Pleasant Grove neighborhood of Southeast Dallas; it is now located in an underserved neighborhood with much of the population living in poverty. In 2000, the dwindling congregation was forced to look at their future. They wondered if the neighborhood would miss them if they closed their doors. Garden Coordinator Becky Smith shares:

We began gathering ideas and praying. How could we take our faith out of the building? How could we live it? How could we serve our neighbors? How could we be a part of the neighborhood?

We had no money, but we did have four acres, a few gardeners, and guidance available from Bill Lambert from Gardeners in Community Development, a local organization that managed the East Dallas Asian Gardens. That was 2000. Our Saviour Church had been put on the Diocese of Dallas's replant list and was told not to begin the garden ministry. Three years later, still on that list, all the growth was north of Dallas.

We are in the underserved food desert of South Dallas. What is the worst that could happen? The garden would go back to grass, but in the meantime it could be planting seeds and feeding people. Bill Lambert was quite surprised, but pleased we were going to begin. We continue our garden ministry/GICD relationship as the teaching site for GICD, the Center for Growing People.[1]

---

1. Becky Smith, e-mail correspondence with author, October 17, 2016.

With an average Sunday attendance of 29 and an annual budget of less than $40,000, this small mission sought to make a difference, give back to the community, and be in God's service despite its seeming lack of resources. With those goals and a partnership for "seed money" and training, Our Saviour Community Garden was established as a donation garden to help with food security by giving families a place to organically grow vegetables. Their dream was to be good stewards of the earth, to plant seeds of hope and faith, and to pass along the gifts they had been given by God.

In the first year the mission's garden donated over one thousand pounds of vegetables to the Southeast Dallas Emergency Food Center. The following year, over one ton was donated. In 2005, through Gardeners in Community Development (GICD), the garden was included in Heifer International's Urban Agriculture Initiative. Heifer funding helped with raised beds, tools, soil amendments, education, seeds, fruit and nut trees, and livestock (worms and bees.) These gifts greatly improved the garden, increasing the gifts to be passed on. The next year, 2006, over two tons (5,500 lb., 22,000 individual servings) were donated, not counting what was used at parishioners' own tables or shared with friends.

Gardeners in Community Development (GICD) is a Dallas area non-profit organization of professionals, volunteers, and supporters of community gardening and neighborhood greening. Incorporated in 1994 for the purpose of promoting community gardening as a way to enhance neighborhood life, its mission is growing people.

Bill Lambert of Gardeners in Community Development writes:

Our Saviour Community Garden was a great leap of faith for an inexperienced small group with scarce resources located in a struggling neighborhood. We were eager to assist this brave effort, so when Our Saviour sought guidance from GICD to till and plant a garden for twenty people, we were excited to serve them. That first year brought together a group of diverse individuals from the community, who not only formed fast friendships but who proudly succeeded in donating 1,546 pounds to their local food pantry. That beginning exceeded their expectations and generated excitement that continues now, twelve years later. Over time, the garden doubled in size, added a fruit orchard, pavilion, greenhouse, and chickens. Since that humble beginning this one group of gardeners has donated over 27 tons to local food pantries, and dozens of neighbors come each week to tend the garden and share its bounty.[2]

On an ecumenical level, Church of Our Saviour has helped eight African American churches in the southern portion of Dallas that share similar concerns of being food deserts for fresh produce. Within the Diocese of Dallas, the congregation has offered assistance to eight Episcopal churches to begin their own community gardens.

With its harvesting and community success, Our Saviour Garden has grown into a GICD teaching garden. School children, science clubs, and vacation Bible schools have come to the garden classroom. Boy Scouts earn service badge requirements by helping harvest. Classes are held on canning, seed saving, composting, and vermiculture. Techniques of repurposing leaves and grass, chopped tree trimmings, old fencing, and kitchen scraps have taught many how to benefit the environment. This education led to the church being awarded the 2006 Hearts of Hope for Environmentalism from the Volunteer Center of North Texas.

Local businesses have also been supportive. The local Wal-Mart awarded a matching grant for their plant sale. J.P. Morgan/Chase Bank and The S.P.A.R.K.S. Foundation donated funds for fencing when a local Master Halco provider offered it at an affordable price within their budget. Starbucks sponsors a plot, workdays, and pickle sales. The Plot Against Hunger is bringing the neighborhood and community together in ways no one expected.

Much has happened since that first desire to serve God and neighbor. The Center for Growing People is now located on the grounds of Our Saviour Episcopal Church. A community gardening training project of the Dallas Urban Gardening Initiative (DUG IN) in partnership with Heifer International, it encompasses indoor classroom space, an outdoor pavilion and water

---

2. From a visit to the Church of Our Saviour Farm, February 25, 2016, by the author and e-mail correspondence with author, October 20, 2016.

catchment structure, fruit orchards, and a vineyard, composting center, and individual plots for families (Saint Saviour's Plot Against Hunger) as well as a community operated farm for food pantry production (Just Greens).

Becky talks about how Our Saviour's gardens are flourishing in 2016:

> We began putting in gardens in home yards, beginning with seniors. We are work-ing with the Parkland Hospital/Aetna Community representative for our area on bringing Pleasant Grove Food Pantry client families to the garden once a month. We introduce them to the garden, organic gardening, and the produce we have donated into their diets. In November we will have them plant garlic and greens in pots to take home; at the next gathering we will pick veggies and herbs and do a little cooking and tasting. And it grows! We are also receiving a LFL, Little Free Library. Ours will include a Seed Bank![3]

More than twenty new community gardens have started in the past couple of years by GICD, predominantly at area churches, most of which have adopted donation policies. The total pounds of fresh vegetables donated to alleviate hunger are much greater than the 3,121 pounds donated in 2015 (the last year numbers were available), as many eat and give away to friends what they grow. Community gardening is making an impact on food security and hunger in the Dallas area.

Prayer keeps Our Saviour grounded. When their local food pantry closed, with God's help they found a way to bring local churches together to open a new pantry, the Pleasant Grove Food Pantry. They established Neighbors in Need to deliver fresh vegetables to those they identified in their neighborhood as homebound or with specific dietary needs. A Jubliee Ministry of the Episco-pal Church, Our Saviour blesses its garden every year on Rogation Sunday, and it blesses those they serve every day.

---

3. Becky Smith, e-mail correspondence with author, October 20, 2016.

"Harvesting Garlic" at the Faith and Grace Garden, St. Timothy's, West Des Moines, Iowa. (*Photo by Marilyn McKinney. Used with permission.*)

14

Composting

The Story of GROW[1]

I grew up in the Rocky Mountains, spent my young adult years in the Great
Plains, where the open spaces and fields of grain formed my faith in the
context of creation, and attended graduate school on the East Coast.
During my first call to parish ministry, I found myself on pastoral visits taking
the "long way" through the back roads and hills of Connecticut—in awe at the
frosty treetops in the winter, the glorious spring buds, the warm sunshine of
summer, or the breathtaking foliage.

In Vermont I found my call in the dirt and hard work of farming. As vicar of
St. Dunstan's, a mission church in the Diocese of Vermont, we met in barns—
working barns, round barns, remodeled barns where the heifer stanchions and
feeding troughs were still in use but now served as baptismal fonts and altar
rails. We shared in the Eucharist of fresh baked bread made from grains grown
in our local soil, honey harvested in local fields, and the wine cured from local
northern grapes. We gathered in circles wearing overalls and ski pants, as some
congregants took a break from farm duties while others grabbed a moment of
reflection before hitting the ski slopes.

Three children, a few chickens, and a flock of sheep later, my family found
our own focus in an unlikely place—in the dark, moist soil beneath the cover
crops in our fields. Each year as our children grew, our gardens and farm
expanded. In the spring, we would seek organic amendments for the short
growing season in Vermont. It was difficult to find compost suitable for organic

---

1. I am grateful to Lisa Ransom for writing this piece. It is used here with her permission.

production. The struggle to amend our soils became the focus of our farming. It became clear over time that the materials we needed to create a perfect compost were right in our backyard—the manures from our chicken and sheep, the food scraps left over from our meals, the carbon from our ongoing forestry management. We also had an abundance of land, the farrow fields.

We had nothing to lose. I could continue to offer my ministry to the church. My husband, Scott, a master mechanic, had the skills to manage the business. Both of us had a deep desire to stay close to our growing family.

Green Mountain Reclaimed Organic Waste (GROW) Compost was born. We started our business with a plan to use the organic resources we saw wasted in our food cycle and our deep desire to connect with our community. We offered a place for neighbors to bring their food scraps. We connected with our local farmers and arranged to pick up their manures and spoiled grain. We built our gardens around this full circle system and invited others to join in our effort. We imagined a community where no one was hungry and no resource was wasted.

In 2012 the state of Vermont passed the Universal Recycling Law that began to prohibit organic material from landfill. It is estimated that 30 to 50 percent of the waste in our landfills is organic material that could be reclaimed and returned to depleted soils. Although this is not as easy as it sounds, we were equipped with the equipment and knowledge to manage large amounts of material, mixing in appropriate ratios and curing the compost to completion before screening and selling back to our farmers. Grow Compost taught us this truth: the regeneration of waste can become rich organic living soil! This was the incarnation of our faith happening right under our feet:

> Once Jesus was asked by the Pharisees when the kingdom of God was coming, and he answered, "The kingdom of God is not coming with things that can be observed; nor will they say, 'Look, here it is!' or 'There it is!' For, in fact, the kingdom of God is among you." (Luke 17:20–21)

Compost is created through the biological activity of microorganisms in decomposing carbon-based material. This decomposition happens naturally in nature over centuries. By combining materials in appropriate ratios of carbon and nitrogen, we can help facilitate this process. By providing a space and communicating our intentions, the material was abundant: food scraps, farm manures, bedding material, silage, hay, grass clippings, leaves, beer brewing residuals, wood chips—all within our own community.

Our daily prayer was simple: *give us this day our daily bread*. And day after day, we watched trucks full of wood chips and bedding pull into the site to drop off their loads to contribute to the process of returning these resources to the soil.

Grow Compost has evolved to a larger role in the management of organic material in the state of Vermont where food scraps have been banned from land-filling in the state. Grow Compost now manages organics throughout the state by hauling unused quality food to those in need, delivering food scraps that are appropriate for animal feed to farms and feedstock, and the rest to anaerobic digesters throughout the state to help facilitate the closed loop of organics back to the food cycle. The Alleluia Fund[2] through the Diocese of Vermont funded a project to connect local communities to the excess food collected through gleaning and food rescue. I [Lisa] have worked to facilitate these connections through local congregations and feeding programs in Central Vermont.

The resilience of our lives depends upon the smallest of creatures: these microorganisms that capture the carbon from the atmosphere and turn it to food for our soils. The more diversity introduced, the healthier and more resil-ient our community becomes. At Grow Compost we focus on manures from animals with different digestive systems (ruminants, horse) to populate our soils with microbes that digest and feed a variety of species, creating a soil that is organically diverse and able to resist disease and stress. Death and distur-bance is the key to fertility and regeneration. God's perfection is reflected in the systems and patterns of nature—from the regenerative food system and the fresh eggs in the barn to the formation of seashells and the cycle of nutrients in our earth's living skin, the soil.

---

2. *http://diovermont.org/alleluia-fund.php.*

"Sister Catherine Grace, Beekeeper" at Bluestone Farm in Brewster, New York (*Photo courtesy of Community of the Holy Spirit. Used with permission.*)

15

The University Farm

The University of the South, Sewanee, Tennessee

Agriculture has long been a part of the ethos of the University of the South in Sewanee, Tennessee. A campus farm was established in 1898 in order to supplement the local food supply for its dining facilities. Until the 1960s, the farm consisted of a dairy, fifteen acres of vegetable production, and both small and large livestock. A resurgent interest in agro-ecology has led to a reactivation of the University Farm. Today it is a teaching tool, complementing the traditional education program by operating as a living laboratory alongside studying the many social, economic, environmental, and political issues related to our natural resources and food supply in the United States.

Colmore Farm, on the Sewanee Plateau, first farmed by Robert Lionel Colmore, bursar and general manager of the University of the South in the 1800s, was purchased by William Claiborne in 1905 for the Order of the Holy Cross, a monastic order in New York, to be a mission school for needy mountain boys. In 2008, **St. Andrew's School** chose to return the farm to its origins and offer a farm program for its students that focuses on sustainability by using crop rotation, interplanting cover crops, and the use of companion planting to create a sustaining ecosystem. Students learn the seed-to-plate process as organic food is now produced for their own dining hall.

The University subsidizes the farm as a learning resource through the Office of Environmental Stewardship and Sustainability. In turn, the farm sells

90 percent of the organic produce to the dining hall at conventional, wholesale prices, as well as eggs and meat. Almost all of the workers and volunteers are University students. Farm manager Carolyn Hoagland writes:

> We provide a setting that enables students to think deeply about their place in the world and to consider how their actions affect the world around them. We do not inquire into the religious beliefs of any worker, volunteer, or partner organization. There are four VISTA/Americorps members who use the farm as their working site. They are helping us with outreach, technology transfer, and the promotion of sustainable agriculture as a method of reducing poverty in our surrounding counties.
>
> There are challenges. We have powerful tractors and tillers on site and we sometimes have large numbers of volunteers with skill sets and interests that vary widely. Our goal is to keep everyone engaged in something useful and interesting, while keeping all their fingers and toes attached. Sometimes this means that high priority and high skill tasks have to be put off for times when fewer people are on site.
>
> We have been surprised at how many people love the goats, while 20 percent are afraid of chickens. And deer often wait until the day before you are ready to harvest—then they eat the whole row.[1]

Today the University Farm has an established organic garden, a flock of fifty laying hens, three beehives, and a herd of seven goats which kid in the spring. A 30 x 95 foot high tunnel greenhouse is under construction. In addition to two summer interns, about 1,000 students volunteer or visit the farm each semester, with an average worker giving 15 to 20 hours per week.

The GreenHouse (which does not have a formal relationship with the University Farm) is an intentional community of eleven students focused on sustainable and creative living and being infectiously joyful. They organize educational events and practice sustainable living by raising chickens and a small garden. This is one of many components of Sustain Sewanee,[2] the University's "green" initiative. The School of Theology has a student-led terrace

---

1. Carolyn Hoagland, e-mail correspondence with author, October 3, 2016.
2. http://sustain.sewanee.edu/.

garden and university students can be part of the Sewanee Beekeeping Society. Other agrarian ministries on the mountain include Otey Memorial Parish, which has an extensive food ministry to the hungry in the greater community.

> The first chaplain at the University of the South was Dr. William Porcher Dubose. He married Mrs. Louise Yerger, one of the founding widows of Fairmont College, a school for girls in nearby Monteagle. Following World War I, this property was acquired for the **DuBose Memorial Church Training School**. It became a place to train "mature men with professional and business experience for rural ministry."[3] The school was a forebear of the School of Theology at Sewanee, with students working on the farm as well as attending class and studying. Today the property is a retreat and conference center in the Diocese of Tennessee.

Other Episcopal-founded universities also are engaged in agricultural sustainability:

- **Kenyon College** in Gambier, Ohio, has an Office of Green Initiatives that helps members of the campus community protect their shared environment. Food for Thought is an initiative to explore food, farming, and rural life. At the Kenyon Farm, pastoral meets academic as students operate the ten-acre farm, living in a house on the property, and managing the care of the animals, including turkeys, goats, and chickens, as well as the growing and harvesting of field crops such as potatoes, basil, and sunflowers.
- **Bard College**, located along the Hudson River in New York, has a student-initiated garden, established in 2012. The 1.5-acre farm allows students to grow food in ways that are ecologically sound, demonstrate the methodologies for sustainable food production, and be responsive to the latest scientific and agricultural practices for growing substantial crops.
- **Voorhees College** located in Denmark, South Carolina, won a 2015 Tier II grant of $10,000 in The Home Depot Retool Your School Competition. The grant proposal involved the creation of a community garden. The purpose of the garden will be to grow fresh vegetables and fruit so that

---

3. *www.duboseconf.org/history* (accessed October 26, 2016).

students, employees, and the community will have access to fresh sustainably grown produce.

- The Trinity Community Garden is an urban community garden started by **Trinity College** in Hartford, Connecticut. Its aim is to strengthen the relationship between the college and the Hartford community. The project, called Fresh Food, New Connections, received a Mellon Grant to execute a plan where a rotating group of faculty members would maintain and utilize the community garden, incorporate an academic focus of studying the economics of farmers' markets, and engage with the local neighboring community. The project provides Hartford families with food security by giving them access to nutritious foods at a reasonable price and by promoting healthy practices. Throughout the summer families grow squash, tomatoes, beans, and other types of produce in raised beds in the garden in order to increase growing capacity.

"Picking Pumpkins" at the Faith and Grace Garden, St. Timothy's, West Des Moines, Iowa (*Photo by Marilyn McKinney. Used with permission.*)

16

Creation Keepers
St. Andrew's Episcopal Church, Seattle, Washington

L ocated in Seattle's Green Lake neighborhood, St. Andrew's has a number of outreach ministries connected to growing food, feeding those in need, and caring for God's creation. Being located in an urban area without any flat areas for gardening as well as a sewer line in need of repair did not stop the willpower and creativity of the Creation Keepers, a group of church members focused on greening the church facility and grounds.

Initially begun as a four-level terraced set of raised beds constructed from scrap lumber and potting soil mixed with the dense clay ground soil, a garden sprouted in 2007. But the following summer a sewer line needed repair, which meant the garden had to be dug up by Seattle Public Utilities (SPU). With a group of skilled volunteers, negotiations with SPU enabled a new and improved garden to be planted, with funds provided by SPU, as well as a grant from the city of Seattle to build a three-stage compost bin. Today you will discover level terraced sets of raised beds that will last twenty years, constructed with a substance called Trex, a composite material used for the construction of decks.

Beginning with a 200-square-foot garden in 2007, 590 square feet was cultivated in 2016, with another 255 set aside for other uses such as composting and storage. The abundance of crops has also grown: bush and climbing peas, red Russian and dino kale, chard, collards, mustard greens, zucchini, all types of squash (yellow crookneck, delicata, butternut, and pumpkin), pole and bush beans, cabbage, five varieties of lettuce, arugula, rhubarb, grapes, thornless blackberries, strawberries, spinach, onions, potatoes, and five varieties of tomatoes. All of this produce is used for a sit-down "Jubilee Dinner" on the last Sunday of each month for those in need, a hot meal for homeless teens in Seattle's University District ("Teen Feed") on the third Wednesday of each month, and a monthly food collection for the local food bank, "FamilyWorks Food Bank." Church dinners also benefit from the garden's abundance: VBS, an annual vestry fundraising meal, the kick-off Sunday church potluck. Members of the congregation, neighbors, and students in a cooking class also benefit.

Volunteers in the garden are very much connected to our activities at St. Andrew's. Youth, Sunday school classes, members of the congregation, and homeless individuals who are connected to the church help with short-term projects, weeding, pruning, and harvesting. In 2010, an AmeriCorps intern helped with environmental issues alongside the Creation Keepers group. A parish capital campaign enabled the hiring of a person to assist in the construction of a garden expansion in 2015. However, much of the efforts of the garden's success can be attributed to J. B. Hoover, a parishioner and volunteer with experience in sustainable gardening and creation care initiatives. While he shares that he has put hundreds of hours of work into the garden, he also acknowledges the "tens of thousands of volunteer worms and billions of microorganisms turning yard and food waste into compost."[1]

Funding comes in small part from St. Andrew's, with some members of the congregation directly contributing to the fund. A grant of $1,000 was received from Seattle Tilth for construction of a Gravity Composting system. Other partners in support have been the Bishop's Committee for the Environment, and Mr. Nguyen Yard Service. Composting is an important piece of the environmental efforts at St. Andrew's and serves as a teaching tool and model for others to follow.

It was discovered that through the various feeding programs hosted by St. Andrew's there were hundreds of pounds of vegetable scraps produced every year. With grant funds from the city of Seattle, "green cones" were purchased and buried near the garden and well-marked waste stations were located on the church property. Youth and children are especially leading the way, making sure all of their events are "green" by using compostable materials. Teaching individuals to recycle is a constant process, but the church's landfill waste has significantly decreased because of these efforts.

---

1. J. B. Hoover, e-mail correspondence with author, September 23 2016

Bishop's Committee for the Environment (BCE) was created to celebrate and heal God's creation by helping churches in the Diocese of Olympia (Western Washington) find ways to make the fifth Mark of Mission—to strive to safeguard the integrity of creation and sustain and renew the life of the earth—part of their ministries. The BCE offers speakers and workshops. It supports churches interested in implementing the Genesis Covenant by training churches to use the EPA's carbon calculator, Portfolio Manager for Houses of Worship. It offers small, competitive Green Grants to jump-start energy-saving projects for church facilities. By networking faith and environment groups throughout the diocese, the Bishop's Committee for the Environment shares information and celebrates the success of our churches.

J. B. Hoover shares his passion:

For me the most important thing to keep in mind about the Garden at St. Andrew's is that it is just one part of an overall approach to environmental stewardship and social justice. It is becoming increasingly clear that our stewardship for the environment is absolutely connected to social justice. When we dump billions of tons of CO_2 pollution into the atmosphere, it is the most vulnerable who suffer the effects of climate change the most. When we fill our yard waste container full of organic material and then later go out and purchase compost or wood chips or mulch, we participate in a system that separates us from some of the most basic aspects of life. Through the work in the garden, we compost nearly 100 percent of our campus yard waste and a growing amount of St. Andrew's food waste. We rehabilitate areas of our campus that were forgotten or considered our own dumping ground, and transform them into beautiful productive spaces. Rather than following other organizations, the church must be a leader in this regard. We must pay especially strict attention to the use of its land and human and financial resources. Within this context, the garden plays a central role, both in transforming the church, but also in transforming the lives of those attend it.[2]

In 2014 St. Andrew's chose to stop watering their grass lawn. This has led to water conservation, since water is only used for the vegetable and flower

2. J. B. Hoover, e-mail correspondence with author, September 23, 2016.

gardens. Yes, the lawn is sometimes brown in the summer, but it remains growing and healthy.

Creation Keepers continue to raise awareness and action for addressing climate change in the parish and have supported the installation of solar panels at
the church. Many opportunities are made available for parishioners to join in
sustainability efforts through links on their church's website. Links include initiatives such as buying carbon offsets, using zipcars and public transportation,
eating locally grown food and shopping at farmers' markets, and more. As a
congregation, they have adopted the Genesis Covenant, which was adopted by
the 2009 General Convention of The Episcopal Church. Through all of their
efforts, they have made "a public commitment to work to reduce greenhouse
gas emissions from every facility it maintains by a minimum of 50 percent
within ten years."[3] In the Diocese of Olympia, this covenant is viewed as part
of one of their three priority areas: congregational development, concentrating
on those aged, and stewardship of all resources, including the earth.

---

3. *http://www.episcopalchurch.org/files/genesis_convenant_final.pdf.*

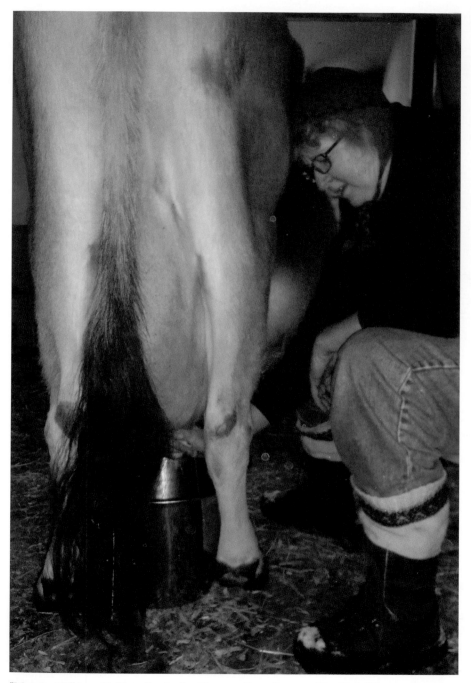

"Morning Milking with Sister Bernice " at Bluestone Farm, Brewster, New York (*Photo courtesy of Community of the Holy Spirit. Used with permission.*)

17

Bluestone Farm

Community of the Holy Spirit, Brewster, New York

The Community of the Holy Spirit is a monastic community for women in the Episcopal Church, and a witness to the work of the Holy Spirit in the world. Founded in 1952, the Community has evolved from its original focus on elementary school teaching to a broader approach to learning that includes education about living sustainably, spiritual direction, retreat leadership, and guest hospitality.

Located in the heart of New York City, around the year 2000 Sister Miriam Therese MacGillis posed the question to the community at St. Hilda's House, "What are all the unborn of the future asking of you that they might come into existence?" In 2003 Sister Heléna Marie and Sister Catherine Grace took that question and moved from the city convent to Brewster, New York (about an hour from St. Hilda's), forming the Melrose Convent with the intent to begin an Earth Literacy Center much like Genesis Farm, an ecological center founded in 1980 as a project of the Dominican Sisters of Caldwell, New Jersey.

They discovered that their circumstances, resources, and surrounding community didn't support such a plan. In the midst of discerning what they were being called to do, they started an herb and vegetable garden on the property and realized that they were very successful at farming. The twenty-three-acre Bluestone Farm was born as part of the Melrose community. Today the farm is based on principles of organic agriculture and animal husbandry, biodynamics, permaculture, and the importance of reskilling for the future. In addition to the gardens, the farm now has chickens, bees, and cows. Bluestone Farm is an ever-evolving entity with its own ethos, personality, and interconnections.

All produce (and milk, honey, and more) is used to feed those on the farm, now averaging about fifteen to twenty people a day. There is an on-site farmers' market, and "overages" are occasionally given to a local feeding program.

Meet the Nuns of Bluestone Farm *www.episcopalchurch.org/page/wayfarer*

Now entering its second decade, the sisters at Melrose are recognizing that their focus is gradually shifting from the hard work of establishing a farm to the work of education. Sister Catherine Grace reflects:

> The farm and our spiritual practice are the core of what is developing into what we think of as a very diverse "eco-community"—interfaith, multigendered, ethnically diverse, and multigenerational. We are building space for, and offering gathering opportunities to, model and share sustainable, resilient living, all of which is essentially grounded in the spiritual life.
>
> I think it is the "multiness" of the growing community here, and particularly the spiritual "piece" that we offer. We find the many young (twenties to thirties) who come here are seeking deep connection with the Divine. Other gatherings have been created and are managed by our partners, who hold frequent "salons"—focused weekend gatherings for young entrepreneurs who want to create purpose-based programs rather than profit-based. Those programs offer a balance of mindfulness practices, farm work, relaxation, and focused conversations.[1]

Financially autonomous, visitors and groups who gather at Bluestone Farm contribute, friends make donations, and the sisters seek grants (although they have been unsuccessful in this area). A recent capital campaign allowed for the renovation of the building that houses the convent. Admittedly not yet self-sustainable, the Sisters of the Holy Spirit bear the brunt of expenses. Partners are thus very important and include: MindKind Institute, Pivotal Leadership, and Prime Produce. All of these organizations have been inspired by and participated in the ethos of Bluestone Farm through offering retreats for themselves and their clientele.

The education offered is not typically in the form of workshops or classroom learning, but is experiential. The sisters call their education "Earth literacy"—learning to care for the earth in the context of the sacredness of all creation. This kind of learning involves putting one's hands in the soil, tending plants, taking care of animals, growing your own food, preserving food for winter, and living the deep

---

1. Sister Catherine Grace, e-mail correspondence with author, August 8, 2016.

rhythms of the cycles of nature, the growing season, and the monastic liturgical year. The lost arts of food preservation, spinning and weaving, cheesemaking, and winemaking show the interconnections with the farm ecosystem.

People come to the farm for a day, a week, or a season. "Farm Companions" are especially invited for the height of the growing season when extra hands are needed. Even as a "temporary" member of the community, visitors participate in the daily worship (including the Divine Office), communal meals, and the work of the farm. It is like a budding eco-village with a permanent monastic core.

Sister Catherine Grace sums up the challenges as well as joys in such a ministry:

> For me, the challenge has been considering the future of the religious life, the future of this beautiful property currently in our care, the future of this planet, and the hope of and for young people. Everything about the land and its inhabitants is filled with surprise (and wisdom); the deepening consciousness of so many young people; the generosity of others (time, assistance, support). . . . I live in a world of surprises, and I love it!

Gardening in Monastic Communities Many of the monastic communities throughout the Episcopal Church have agricultural initiatives. Brother Bernard Delcourt is a beekeeper and permaculture farmer at **Holy Cross Monastery**, an Anglican Benedictine Community of Men in West Park, New York. Emery House, a retreat center part of the ministry of the **Society of St. John the Evangelist** located north of Boston, has an organic farm as part of their life, with more than an acre of intensive vegetable production, some small grains, and two hundred laying hens, broilers, and turkeys. The food produced feeds the Society and its guests, is donated to a local food shelter, and is distributed through a small CSA and farm stand. The **Southern Province of the Sisterhood of St. Mary** in Sewanee, Tennessee, community has developed flower gardens, an organic vegetable garden, fruit orchards, and a prayer garden. They have recently begun a partnership to grow lavender for Thistle Farms. Good Earth Farm is located in Athens, Ohio, where **The Common Friars**, an emerging monastic order of men and women, married and single, lay and ordained, seek to understand and live out what it means to be a Christian disciple today. They place the utmost importance on being connected to the land, to each other, and to those on the margins of society. Their three-acre farm produces enough food to sustain itself and some local food pantries.

"Pollinator Program Tagged Butterfly" at the Faith and Grace Garden, St. Timothy's, West Des Moines, Iowa (*Photo by Marilyn McKinney. Used with permission.*)

18

Faith and Grace Garden

St. Timothy's Episcopal Church, West Des Moines, Iowa

Over the past fourteen years, hundreds of volunteers from dozens of religious congregations, schools, community groups, Boy Scout groups, and more have come under the guidance, wisdom, and grace of Mark Marshall. In the beginning Mark, a member of St. Timothy's for the past twenty five years, tended the garden in the evenings after walking seven to nine miles each day as a postman. He describes the garden as starting out "small—fifteen to twenty tomato plants, fifteen to twenty pepper plants and another section of twelve or so double rows of peas."[1] After Sunday services, he could be found giving fresh vegetables away to church members and later distributing the remaining produce to needy parishioners who were not present that day, especially elderly people who had trouble getting to the store.

Today the church's vision and mission is "to feed all God's people." Located on four acres in-between St. Timothy's Episcopal Church and Covenant Presbyterian Church in West Des Moines, Iowa, Mark shares:

> The best year yielded eight tons! This year we will harvest over 5,000 pounds of tomatoes, with the best night of tomato picking yielding 660 pounds—that is a lot of marinara.[2]

One of the biggest challenges faced by church-based garden ministries is finding volunteers. It is a task that goes beyond the congregation: the sustainability of a food ministry means looking beyond the volunteer parishioner. And

1. Mark Marshall, e-mail correspondence with author, October 7, 2016.

2. Ibid.

the Faith and Grace Garden has much to teach others about how to open up this ministry to the wider community. Begun as part of the parish's community ministries commission, it began with a garden of less than one thousand square feet and twelve parishioners. It has now grown in size and is joined by fifty volunteers from outside the church comprised of friends, neighbors, and passersby. Nearby churches send volunteers too.

Four years ago Meutia Hakim was a foreign exchange student at Valley High School in West Des Moines and a Faith and Grace Garden volunteer. Earning a scholarship from the Wallace Foundation, she participated in the Real Soil, Real Food, A Real Difference summer program that helps develop leadership and problem-solving skills and increases students' knowledge base for potential careers in agriculture, food science, health and wellness, social services, environmental studies, and other areas. Now back home in Indonesia, she is majoring in food technology at Surya University. Today, local high school students fulfill their community service hour requirements or participate for a variety of volunteer experiences.

Ashworth Road Baptist Church has a team of volunteers that work in the garden every Wednesday during the growing season. Part of their team is Mary Fraser, eighty-four, who brings hundreds of pounds of vegetables from her home garden when she comes to work in the Faith and Grace Garden. Recently honored as the 2016 Volunteer of the Year, her homegrown produce is added to the Faith and Grace Garden shipment to the local food pantries.

Lutheran Social Services in Iowa provide garden volunteers from Bhutan and Burma who work together, share food and fellowship, and teach us about the health and nutritional benefits of many of the native plants that grow in and around the garden while they practice their English. They work together for a couple of hours, then snack on some fruit in the shade.

Keeping in touch with volunteers has helped in their retention. E-mail informs them of needs: planting, watering, weeding, harvesting, and delivering vegetables to the local food pantries and the area food bank. Communication with volunteers as well as learning more about those who receive the produce for their families has helped determine what should be grown also. Learning about the culture and dietary preference of food pantry clients has changed what is grown: hot peppers, tomatillos, cilantro, collard greens, mustard greens, sweet potatoes, and fava beans would otherwise never had been considered as crops.

Grow the Food is a collection of five community gardens in the Des Moines area with the goal of growing food to feed the local hungry. Their website helps coordinate the efforts of faith gardens, including the sharing of resources and communication to volunteers. In 2016, over fifteen thousand pounds of food was jointly donated to food distribution centers from these gardens. See *www.growthefood.org*.

Mark plans to retire as a postal worker in 2017 and hopes to make the garden his full-time job. And the garden continues to grow:

> This spring we converted two of our six flowerbeds into pollinator gardens with the guidance of the Polk County Conservation Department, which received a federal grant to provide the plant sets. If all goes well, I believe they will provide us with enough plant sets to convert at least two more beds and maybe even all four, but we'll see. The blueberry bushes are coming along great, but they are slow growers, so it will be a few years before we are at full capacity, which should eventually be 1,000 to 1,500 lbs. I would like to plant another fifty bushes next year or the year after.[3]

Through their support and empowerment of Mark Marshall and the commitment to the ministry of Faith and Grace, St. Timothy's reaches deep into their community and brings life into the parish. A Boy Scout connects through his Eagle project, a neighbor is able to keep bees on the property, and the Master Gardeners of Iowa come to learn and be inspired.

Master Gardeners are a thread that weaves in and out of this book. Many of our volunteers are both master gardeners (individuals in the community who are not certified, but are considered to be "masters" at gardening) and Master Gardeners (certified by the county extension). Both types have a tendency of "hiding their light under a bushel." The Episcopal Church and our neighbors are filled with green thumbs. . . . I have learned that you don't have to ask your local Master Gardeners twice for help. Master Gardener programs, usually run through county extension programs, are volunteer programs that train people in the science and art of gardening. In turn, the Master Gardeners take the information they learn during the training and advise and educate the public on gardening and horticulture.

---

3. Mark Marshall, e-mail correspondence with author, October 7, 2016.

"A Farmer-Priest Offers a Blessing" at Church of the Holy Cross in Redmond, Washington (*Photo ourtesy of Jim Eichner. Used with permission.*)

19

Food Bank Farm
Church of the Holy Cross, Redmond, Washington

I t began with a love affair with a neighbor's family farm in Cedarburg, Wisconsin, when he was two years old. By the time he was eight, Jim had daily duties on the farm that included greeting the pigs, ducks, chickens, cattle, dogs, and cats after school. In high school he realized that his dream of becoming a farmer would never materialize—farms were closing due to bankruptcy or merging into big, corporate conglomerations. But still he put in his three-hours-a-day chores of greeting the livestock, downing a ton of hay, rolling six one hundred-pound bags of feed, forking hay for the heifers, collecting three hundred eggs, prepping the milk machines, scraping manure out of the stalls, and laying down lime on the ground, followed by the tenth of a mile walk home in the dark. Jim learned about pride and what it meant to be entrusted with caring for a farm.

Today Jim Eichner is the rector of Church of the Holy Cross and overseer of Food Bank Farm and outreach of the three hundred–member parish in Redmond, Washington. Following a sabbatical in 2009 where he spent three months volunteering at Jubilee Biodynamic Farm in nearby Carnation, he realized he was still competent and there was no going back. He could be a priest and a farmer. He recognized that he was "culturally conditioned" during his childhood:

> Everything I do in running and managing a church is based on what I learned on that German family farm. It was the behavioral patterning of seasonality, harvesting, and working as a team. Theologically, a priest/farmer can see how people are

connected and understand how the church is a vector of benevolence. We have the infrastructure. We see the need. We can help people connect to one another in the community. I said "yes" to God and let God do the rest.[1]

Before Food Bank Farm began, Jim developed a relationship with Clean Greens, a small, nonprofit organic market founded and operated by New Hope Missionary Baptist Church in Seattle. He met Tommie Willis, who is the farm manager for Clean Greens—it turns out that farm is only seven miles from Jim's home. God again was helping make the connections. Jim apprenticed under Tommie until it was time to put into action one of his dreams: starting his own farm that would send fresh produce directly to food banks so they wouldn't have to depend on the leftover surplus from other farms.

St. Columba's Just Garden, in Kent, Washington, is one of the ways the congregation forms their faith and connects to God through the resource of the land. The Garden Guild works together to grow and harvest fresh vegetables and fruit to give away at their Emergency Food Bank. They also grow flowers to adorn the worship space, and wheat to make flour for their home-baked communion bread: the gifts of God, for the people of God.

Begun on rented fields (and farm equipment) from Chinook Farms in Snohomish with the purpose of growing their own food, in 2011 twelve volunteers from Holy Cross harvested 3,750 pounds of produce for Clean Greens food banks. After this first successful harvest, local agencies, recognizing that this was not a priest's pipedream but a reality that worked, began to pitch in. Food Lifeline provides bins and trucks to get food from the fields to the distribution warehouse. Local corporations also jumped on board and a financial commitment from across the community allowed Food Bank Farm to scale up, increasing the acreage and volunteer base.

---

1. Jim Eichner, interview with author, October 31, 2016 at Church of the Holy Cross in Redmond, Washington.

On the other side of the Kent Valley is the **Saint James Giving Garden**. They are responding to the need in its diverse, suburban, formerly rural community by starting with several raised beds. The garden has grown with help from the United Thank Offering and an intern who works nearby at Seattle Tilth Farm Works.[2] The garden provides not only fresh produce for the over 1,500 guests who visit the outreach center every year, but also as an opportunity for learning as nearby Title One schools, the church's preschool children, and parish volunteers are engaged. Offerings from the garden are brought to the altar during Eucharist, reminding the gathered faithful about the importance of preserving God's abundant creation.

Holy Cross provides $7,000 a year for rent, fuel, and other expenses not covered by donations. Schools, scouting groups, food bank volunteers, sports teams, businesses, and corporations (such as All-State, Nordstrom, Microsoft, Liberty Mutual, and AT&T) in addition to the parishioners at Holy Cross provide the volunteer hours of planting and harvesting. The United Way of King County is a big supporter in many ways. In 2016, 152,866 pounds of fresh food was harvested from twelve acres with over 1,000 volunteers having logged hours during the year. They held "Harvest Days" in which one corporate partner (AT&T) brought 300 people to pick 40,000 pounds of food in two hours. Jim estimates that in 2016, 611,464 servings of food were donated, valued at $229,299. Food is donated to many area food banks.

Jim continues to have dreams. You can find him driving his tractor two days a week in the fields, planning what they can do with twenty acres in the future. They have the infrastructure, the volunteers, and the supply chain to grow 1 million pounds of produce by 2021—a field of dreams feeding the multitudes in the Seattle area.

---

2. *www.seattletilth.org.*

"Red Door Vineyard" at Church of the Epiphany, Agoura Hills, California (*Photo courtesy of Melissa McCarthy. Used with permission.*)

20

Vineyards and Wheat Fields
The Red Door Vineyard and Honoré Farm and Mill

The Episcopal Church of the Epiphany is a mission congregation of the Diocese of Los Angeles in Agoura Hills. Planted in 1980, the mission church's founders dreamed of planting a biblical garden consisting of oranges, rosemary, figs, pomegranates, and more. Years later two unconnected events occurred that brought that dream to life.

It all started at a bishop's committee annual retreat, which included Bible study with various groups reading different passages of Scripture. When comparing their reflections, it was noted that a theme of vines and vineyards ran through them all. What were they being called to spiritually plant as a mission of the church? On an unrelated note, after rehearsal each week, choir members would share a glass of wine, bringing a social component to their time together. One member of the choir had recently retired from his job as a vintner in Napa Valley. There was also a property concern: behind the church was a steep, large hillside that was home to weeds and brush that needed to be mowed down every June per orders of the local fire department. What to do? Plant a vineyard.

Red Door Vineyard (RDV), a co-op program of Epiphany began soon after. Theological metaphors became a concrete idea when two hundred root-stock of grapes were planted. Its mission is to support and cultivate their community through working the soil, tending vines, harvesting grapes, and carting wine. Vicar Melissa McCarthy shares how the co-op works:

> We don't sell the wine we bottle—we invited individuals in the parish, community, and diocese to purchase shares to be part of the bounty of the harvest. In

addition to the typical three bottles of wine, guild members enjoy other community benefits, including special food, wine, social and educational events, and occasional outings. Based on their gifts of time and/or talents, all workers who labor on behalf of the RDV ministry become Guild members, regardless of their financial contributions. A minimum of 10 percent of the wine produced each year is tithed for use by the church. All funds raised are used to support the vineyard and are given back to the church for its other mission and ministries.[1]

Today Red Door Vineyard Guild members work together to dig, tend, trim, weed, harvest, and crush, all the while deepening and exploring their connection to their inner selves, their neighbors, their community, the earth, and the universe. Red doors have always been a symbol of safety and refuge. At The Church of the Epiphany, they continue to stand for welcome, forgiveness, reconciliation, and spiritual healing as grapes are grown and tended and working together matters.

Wine is one component of the Eucharist; bread is the other. At Honoré Farm and Mill, founder Elizabeth DeRuff currently plants heirloom wheat to be used for communion bread at the Bishop's Ranch, a 350-acre Episcopal retreat center in Healdsburg, California. Named for St. Honoré, the French patron saint of bakers and pastry chefs, its mission is to be a "working farm with a mobile mill house that connects people to food, land, and each other, providing research and education for people to learn to grow and teach others about the sources of their daily bread, as well as preparing them to steward the land upon which it grows."[2] Since its founding in 2014, it has grown from a quarter to a full acre with further plans of growth through a recently successful Kickstarter campaign to build a mobile mill house. They currently grow a variety of heirloom wheat; stone-ground flour is very digestible, so people with gluten sensitivity (not celiac) find they can once again enjoy bread. Honoré Farm and Mill was able to provide all of the Staff of Life Flour that was used by Eva's Bakery in Salt Lake City to supply the communion bread used at the nine daily Eucharists of the 2015 General Convention.

---

1. Melissa McCarthy, phone interview with author, November 9, 2016.

2. *http://honoremill.org/our-mission/*.

Honoré Farm and Mill is a leader in a growing movement of putting local, organic, and sustainable bread on our altar tables. There is a growing understanding that much of the wheat we consume is far from healthy. As a sacramental faith that proclaims the bread of life, we need to make sure the bread we serve is life-giving—spiritually and physically. Honoré Farm and Mill has a "Farm to Altar Table" CSA program of fresh stone-ground flour that is delivered to churches quarterly.

"Planting a Future" in Faubourg Delassize, New Orleans (*Photo courtesy of Holly Heine. Used with permission.*)

21

Greening a Neighborhood
Jericho Road's Orchard and Gardens,
New Orleans, Louisiana

C entral City is one of the neediest parts of New Orleans. Its neighborhoods are full of empty lots where weeds grow rampant. But scattered
among this economically challenged area are signs of hope—many
due to the efforts of Jericho Road Episcopal Housing Initiative. Begun as a
ministry of Christ Church Cathedral in partnership with Episcopal Relief and
Development, this nonprofit organization is now a leading neighborhood-based
community developer working to revitalize neighborhoods by fostering human
capacity that promotes positive change. Change happens by connecting residents with one another, lifting up leaders within the neighborhood, and supporting neighborhood associations. Their housing development program
creates healthy, energy efficient, accessible, and affordable housing. They have
also developed some solutions to the citywide problem of blighted structures
and vacant lots through property acquisition, high-impact lot greening, and
urban agriculture projects.

In 2007 a lot measuring 57 feet by 150 feet and surrounded by apartment
buildings was purchased by Jericho Road. Struggling to keep the lot free of
debris, even after a group fenced it off, Jericho Road began to formulate and
implement their vacant lot greening strategy. Vegetable gardens and an urban
orchard were high on their list as they sought other properties, so they found
partners and funding to make it happen. Alison Ecker, a Grinnell Corps Volunteer for Jericho Road in 2010, wrote on the Pennsylvania Horticultural Society's blog about their progress and hopes:

We've implemented a passive strategy (demolition, mowing, fencing, and trees) on nine properties and have started alternative strategies on four others. This includes a community garden that's already in its second harvest; a potential KaBoom! Playground for which we're being strongly considered; a property that has been entered into the Communities Take Root fruit-tree orchard competition . . . and finally a Tulane City Center garden installation that will first be shown at the New Orleans Botanical Garden's fall show.

This sort of work is very necessary for our neighborhood, and we've already experienced huge advantages in terms of improving visual appearances, deterring dumping, outreaching to residents, and improving neighborhood pride.[1]

The Saratoga Street Fruit Orchard was one of twenty-five winners nationwide in that competition, receiving votes from all over the United States. After the land had been cleared by volunteers, over thirty citrus, persimmon, and fig trees were planted on the lot aided by a donation from Communities Take Root, a program sponsored by Edy's® Fruit Bars and the Fruit Tree Planting Foundation.[2] Holly Heine, director of operations and communications for Jericho Road, says that hands-on learning is a key goal of the project. She also sees the orchard as a means to another very important end: building bonds among neighbors while bringing healthy food and programs where they are needed most. She shares:

> After the initial phases were completed, the orchard is the residents' to tend to and manage. It is up to them what happens to it and they will be the ones making the decisions about how to manage it and how to distribute the produce. Turning vacant lots into community gardens and urban farms and orchards just makes sense in a community like ours and all are innovative ways to attack blight and build community. These are part of Jericho Road's "healthy initiative" programs.[3]

This urban orchard has introduced children in the neighborhood to fresh produce that they may have never had before. Activities centered in the orchard's garden have included the growing of pumpkins and other vegetables.

---

1. *https://phsblog.org/2010/08/24/new-orleans-fight-against-blight/.*

2. *http://www.ftpf.org.*

3. Holly Heine, phone interview with author, November 14, 2016.

Tulane University medical and culinary students have partnered with the community to offer cooking classes for adults, as well as taste testing for children; grilled veggie pizzas were a bit hit! In 2016, thanks to a United Thank Offering grant along with the Episcopal Diocese of Louisiana, the Saratoga Street Fruit Tree Orchard got funds for a new shed. It will provide shading for workers as well as a place to keep tools and supplies used for tending the trees as well as community events that take place in the orchard/garden.

These neighborhood initiatives sparked by Jericho Road continue to spread. Under the leadership of their Green Faith coordinator, Scott Webster—a former Young Adult Episcopal Service Corps member from a different New Orleans project—partnerships are developing with neighbors. Kim Washington, who joined Jericho Road in 2012, believes this is more than about greening the neighborhoods. She believes:

> We need to introduce children to healthy food and eating habits at an early age. This leads to a trajectory through their lives. Thirty percent of the children in New Orleans are living with food insecurity. What started as neighborhood revitalization has turned into providing access to the basic necessities of life to people here.
>
> We are not only teaching children (and adults) to grow food, we are helping them have a healthy relationship to food—to understand where food comes from, the labor that goes in to bringing it to harvest, and what is important to put into your body. We are offering affordable and nutritious food for neighborhoods that are food deserts.
>
> The beautification of these empty lots has led to a reduction in crime in our neighborhoods. When we keep these properties well maintained, there is less dumping and more pride.[4]

Partnering with entities such as Second Harvest Food Bank is teaching neighbors how to cook, how to read labels at the grocery store, and that it is possible to eat healthy on an affordable budget. The Friends of Faubourg (neighborhood) Delassize, Friends of Faubourg Lafayette, Jericho Road Episcopal Housing Initiative, and HandsOn New Orleans have partnered to launch the beautification projects in each faubourg. The program provides volunteers

---

4. Kim Washington, phone interview with author, November 14, 2016.

to work on beautification projects in neighborhoods, to offer minor repair and beautification services to community members, to engage local volunteers in community-building and antiblight efforts, and to make the community more beautiful. This can be seen in neighbors constructing their own gardens, raising chickens in the backyard, and even trying hydroponics at home. Kim shared a story of one woman who has been planting "guerilla gardens" along sidewalks in her neighborhood.

The stories go on and on. Community gardens are springing up. Cooking and food classes are being offered at a local senior center. Entrepreneurs are budding too—growing and selling flowers. Where weeds once grew, hope now grows.

"Girls and Chickens" at Camp Stevens, Julian, California (*Photo courtesy of Ashley Graham-Wilcox. Used with permission.*)

22

Bellwether Farm

A Diocesan Camp and Retreat Farm,
Wakeman Township, Ohio

In 2014, Bishop Mark Hollingsworth challenged the Episcopal Diocese of Ohio to begin a new initiative about how the diocese can be fed, learn, and grow spiritually as well as physically by growing food. His call to action was embraced across the churches and a fundraising campaign was begun to see if it could be a reality, not just in words, but also in financial capital. From 2014 to 2015, the "Planting for Tomorrow: Growing in Faith Today" campaign raised more than $19 million, well beyond the goal of $12 million. Almost $10 million of that will stay in the twenty seven parishes that ran collaborative campaigns with the diocese, and over $9 million will go toward creating a new camp and retreat center to live out this new mission.

On May 1, 2015, 137 acres in Wakeman Township, Ohio, was purchased. Once a working farm that had become a recreational park since 1975, it is now becoming a new camp and retreat center, geographically centered within the diocese. Site construction began in July 2016, with plans for a four-week summer camp program to launch in 2017.

Katie Ong-Landini, project manager, is excited about the future, as building plans are being approved and contractors hired to begin the work. Programs are already occurring on the site, with special days offered to engage adults, youth, and children in a taste of what will be part of what is now being called Bellwether Farm. Katie states:

This will be a working farm, a place where all ages can come to connect our health and wellness with our spirituality. How and what we eat is so important. How do we integrate agrarian ministry into our church ministries and help younger generations learn how to steward the environment in their home community? By coming to Bellwether Farm they will experience and learn how to grow produce and care for the land. They can then take this home to recreate in their own context—school, home, neighborhoods—while learning how to care for creation as well as take care of their neighbors.[1]

She described a recent day in which activities for children and youth involved veggie taste tests, herb identification, soil examination studies, planting herbs in egg cartons to take home, and hikes around the property. In 2017, plans are underway to plant apple trees on a youth and family workday to extend the orchard that already exists onsite. In June the workday will be about constructing thirty Amish worship benches. The materials for the benches will be recycled from lumber that was purchased from an old barn nearby. Livestock will slowly become part of the future also. There are already two beehives and chickens will come soon. Perhaps to be followed by sheep, goats, hogs, and maybe a cow or two.

Why Bellwether? Since the Middle Ages, shepherds have singled out one ram in a flock to wear a bell and indicate where the flock is going. The bellwether has come to signify a harbinger or herald of what is to come. In this sense, it is the Church's vocation to be a bellwether of the kingdom of God, and the vocation of every Christian is to be a bellwether of God's mission to heal the world. It is, of course, our common prayer that through this new camp, retreat, and education center, and in each of our lives, we will be the bellwether of Christ's redeeming and reconciling love.[2]

The plan is to have the farm fully functional in 2018. The vision for this new camp and retreat center is ambitious. Facilities will eventually include

---

1. Katie Ong-Landini, phone interview with author, November 17, 2016.

2. http://dohiocampandretreatfarm.com.

seasonal cabins for ninety-six campers and thirty-two staff members; a farmstead with staff housing, animal and equipment barns, and gardens for children and adults to learn and work. There will be a central dining and program facility for all program participants, a chapel, meeting rooms, and a teaching kitchen. For retreats there will be overnight accommodations for forty. For recreation there will be a five-acre swimming pond and playing fields. All buildings will use renewable energy and sustainable technologies that will also serve as teaching models. All facilities will meet Americans with Disabilities Act (ADA) standards and be accessible to anyone with mobility challenges.

Their goals are also mighty. Besides being a place to foster and develop community through the integration of service, learning, worship, and recreation, Bellwether Farm will be a place to deepen and enrich spiritual practices in an innovative model built around sustainable farming and standards of environmental stewardship. Organic farming will be practiced. Year-round educational opportunities, including partnering with regional farmers, schools, colleges, and environmental organizations, will be offered. A long-term goal is for the farm to produce 50 percent of all the vegetables consumed by guests and staff and 75 percent of all food consumed on site will be from regional sources. Recreational and educational planning will preserve and enhance the wildlife habitats that already exist on the property.

Bishop Hollingsworth shared his vision, which is now becoming a reality. He speaks of how summer camp experiences are life changing. His hope is that Bellwether Farm will be a place to "get away, be in prayer with the companionship of Jesus, live in community where service is central, and lifelong learning and Christian formation is at its heart."[3]

---

3. *https://www.youtube.com/watch?v=r-RdZCVMCqA.*

"Malvern Sheep" at St. Peter's in the Great Valley churchyard in Malvern, Pennsylvania (*Photo by Melford "Bud" Holland. Used with permission.*)

23

Cemeteries
Green Spaces for Growth

Historically the most common use of churchyards was as a consecrated burial ground known as a graveyard. Graveyards were usually established at the same time as the building of the relevant place of worship (which can date back to the sixth through fourteenth centuries in Europe) and were often used by those families who could not afford to be buried inside or beneath the place of worship itself.

The custom of churchyard burial seems to have been suggested by the practice of the monastic orders, who desired to have the bodies of those of their community as near to them as possible, for they were considered in an exceptional sense as very closely united to the living of their order. Once started, it very quickly spread, as we can see from all the churches in Europe and many of the early churches in America where the churchyard remained the most common burial place through the end of the 1800s. By the 1900s the idea of a garden cemetery spread across America as an answer to the old, overcrowded burial grounds. As time has gone by, some churchyard cemeteries remain active with new internments, while others have taken on more historical significance.

We all know churches that carefully manicure their graveyards as well as those that have headstones fallen over and covered with weeds. Some of our churchyards have famous people buried in them, while most have everyday people who were members of the congregation. Churchyards and their graveyards are now also hosts to gardens that produce more than ivy and flowers. Here are a few examples:

London Ferrell Community Garden

"Located four city blocks north of Christ Church Cathedral in Lexington, Kentucky, lies the Old Episcopal Burying Ground. Within its walls rest the cathedral's saints from 1830 to 1870. The cemetery land is rich with history, including the story of African-American Baptist minister London Ferrell. During the cholera epidemic of 1833, Ferrell befriended the dean of Christ Church. They both tended to the dying and both lost wives to the disease. As a great friend to Christ Church, London Ferrell and his family were buried with the cathedral dean within the grounds. Adjacent to the burying ground lies the former Catholic burying ground—two acres of green space within downtown Lexington. When the Catholic Church built a new cemetery in the 1870s, the bodies were exhumed and moved to new ground. Christ Church purchased the adjacent property in 2000 and in 2007 the church was approached by Seedleaf, a local urban gardening organization wanting to farm on the old Catholic cemetery.

For the past seven years, the London Ferrell Garden has supplied fresh vegetables and farm plots to Lexington's poorest residents, serving as a place of racial and social economic reconciliation between church and community and defining the cathedral's mission within the community. In addition to housing the church's saints, the land now houses a community labyrinth. The land and chapel have hosted neighborhood meetings, church picnics, community picnics, wellness clinics, education events, Earth Day celebrations, youth groups, and community organizations. Across time and across denominational boundaries, race, socioeconomics, fed and unfed, the land stretches the Good News of Christ beyond all divisions in downtown Lexington."[1]

Sheep!

St. Peter's in the Great Valley in Malvern, Pennsylvania, has been home to a resident flock of sheep since 2003. Sheep appear all throughout Scripture, best personified for us in the verse from Psalm 100: "We are his people, and the sheep of his pasture." The headstones within the original cemetery walls couldn't withstand the wear and tear of modern-day lawn equipment, so sheep

---

1. Amanda Musterman, "London Ferrell Community Garden" (paper for LTCM 627: Liturgical Time, School of Theology: Sewanee, The University of the South, Fall 2016 term). Used with permission.

have provided the perfect solution: they're the resident lawn mowers, fertilizers, and weed eaters, playing a very important role at St. Peter's in helping to maintain an environmentally and historically friendly lawn care program. The current St. Peter's flock is a crossbred mix, which includes Southdown, Dorset, and Leicester (pronounced "Lester") Longwool breeds. The sire of the St. Peter's flock can trace his heritage to the Leicester Longwools included in Colonial Williamsburg's Rare Breeds program. St. Peter's sheep are provided through the generosity of Colonel and Mrs. Robert Wiltshire.

Natural Burials

More individuals are beginning to consider how their mortal remains are interred and impact the environment. A "green burial" is when one's remains are returned to the earth as directly and simply as possible. It thus avoids embalming (and its toxic chemicals), metal caskets, and burial vaults that are standard features of the modern burial. Simple coffins are made of cardboard or softwoods, like pine, and they are laid to rest into vault-free graves, often in a woodland setting available in the "natural cemeteries" that are beginning to appear around the United States. Becca Stevens, of Thistle Farms fame in Nashville, is part of this movement in Tennessee. While this book can't cover the scope of this topic, you can read about Tennessee's first conservation cemetery promoting natural burial in "How Natural Burial Can Conserve Land in Tennessee."[2]

Growing vegetables, trees, and flowers on top of where our bodies rest is another way to view the life cycle. We are dust and we will return to dust. Out of the dirt comes new life; our remains nourish the earth instead of being entombed inside a casket and vault. In our Ash Wednesday liturgy, as ashes are about to be imposed, we hear:

> Almighty God, you have created us out of the dust of the earth: Grant that these ashes may be to us a sign of our mortality and penitence, that we may remember that it is only by your gracious gift that we are given everlasting life; through Jesus Christ our Savior. Amen.[3]

---

2. *www.tennessean.com/story/news/religion/2016/10/26/how-natural-burial-can-conserve-land-middle-tennessee/91750126/* (accessed December 8, 2016).

3. The Book of Common Prayer, 265.

"Boats and Beds" at St. Andrew's in Fullerton, California. (*Photo courtesy of Linda Drake.*)

24

A Eucharistic Prayer in the Garden[1]
Giving Thanks to God

Kathleen Bean is an Anglican Studies Certificate student currently enrolled at Church Divinity School of the Pacific. She is interning at St. Andrew's Episcopal Church in Fullerton, California, where they have used the hulls of wooden rowboats for their raised garden beds. As part of her studies, Kathleen has written this eucharistic prayer, which is shared here with her permission. It is fitting that we conclude these stories of gardens, feeding, and growth with giving thanks to God, from whom our abundant harvests come.

The people remain standing. The Presider, whether bishop or priest, stands behind the Holy Table, facing the people, throughout, and sings or says:

	The Lord be with you.
People	And also with you.
Presider	Lift up your hearts.
People	We lift them to the Lord.
Presider	Let us give thanks to God our Creator.
People	It is right to give God thanks and praise.

The Presider continues

Praise to you, our gracious God! You created for us a home in your Garden, giving to us a place of bounty and beauty, of nourishment for our bodies and delight for all our senses; a place where we meet you in the songs of birds and the hum of insects, the warming sun and cooling rain, the scent of ripe fruit and the pungent aroma of herbs. You show us your overflowing love with the gift of abundant variety in all the foods that come forth from the soil. Therefore we praise you, joining our voices with all creatures and growing things, and with all the company of heaven, who praise you endlessly in this hymn:

Presider and People

> Holy, holy, holy Lord, God of power and might,
>
> heaven and Earth are full of your glory.
>
> > Hosanna in the highest.
>
> Blessed is the one who comes in the name of the Lord.
>
> > Hosanna in the highest.

The people remain standing.

Then the Presider continues

Creator God, in your great love you made for us this wondrous Earth and entrusted us with its care. You gave us everything we could wish. But our spiritual ancestors rebelled against you, as we ourselves do, and lost their home in your Garden, no more to walk with you in companionship in the evening. For generations you called your people to return to you, and for generations they came and went, until at last, in your mercy, you sent Jesus, your Son, to be born of a woman and join us in our humanity. Jesus fed people's bodies and souls, breaking bread with sinners, feeding the multitudes out of his compassion, celebrating joyful occasions with food and wine. He gave himself as a perfect sacrifice for the world, and rose again that we might live, enlivened by the Holy Spirit, and one day dine with him at the heavenly banquet. Through him, you invite us to return to the Garden.

At the following words concerning the bread, the Presider is to hold it, or lay a hand upon it; and at the words concerning the cup, to hold or place a hand upon the cup and any other vessel containing wine to be consecrated.

On the night before his death, Jesus shared a last meal with his friends. He took a loaf of bread, and when he had given thanks to you, he broke it and gave it to the disciples, saying, "Take, eat: This is my Body, which is given for you. Do this for the remembrance of me."

After supper he took the cup of wine; and when he had given thanks, he gave it to them, and said, "Drink this, all of you: this is my Blood of the new Covenant, which is shed for you and for many for the forgiveness of sins. Whenever you drink it, do this for the remembrance of me."

Therefore we proclaim the mystery of faith:

Presider and People

Christ has died.

Chris is risen.

Christ will come again.

The Presider continues

And now, Creator God, we offer these gifts of the Earth, nourished by sun and rain, transformed by human hands into bread and wine. Sanctify them by your Holy Spirit, to be for us the Body and Blood of our Lord Jesus Christ. Sanctify us also, that empowered by the Spirit we may take your love into our suffering world. Bless this garden, we pray, that it may bring forth abundant food and serve as a living witness of your love and grace. At the last day gather us with all creation into the joy of your eternal kingdom.

All this we ask through Jesus Christ. By him, and with him, and in him, in the unity of the Holy Spirit all honor and glory is yours, now and forever. *AMEN.*

Appendix A
Glossary

apiary: "An apiary (also known as a bee yard) is a place where beehives of honey bees are kept. Traditionally beekeepers (also known as apiarists) paid land rent in honey for the use of small parcels. Some farmers will provide free apiary sites, because they need pollination, and farmers who need many hives often pay for them to be moved to the crops when they bloom. It can also be a wall-less, roofed structure, similar to a gazebo."[1]

aquaponics: A system of aquaculture in which the waste produced by farmed fish, or other aquatic animals, supplies nutrients for plants grown hydroponically, which in turn purify the water.

communal garden: Same as a community garden, except all the produce grown is given to others.

community garden: A plot of land that is gardened by a group of people to produce fruits, vegetables, flowers, and sometimes chickens for egg production. Community gardens exist in a variety of settings, urban and rural, on vacant lots, at schools or community centers, or on donated land. Food may be grown communally, or individuals or families may have their own individual garden plots or beds.

compost: An organic soil amendment resulting from the decomposition of organic material.

cover crop: A crop which is planted in the absence of normal crop to control weeds and add humus to the soil when it is plowed in prior to regular planting.

Community Supported Agriculture (CSA): Community Supported Agriculture creates a direct connection between farmers and consumers. To join a CSA is to buy a share of the season's harvest. The farmer gains the security of knowing he or she has been paid for a portion of the harvest and the farmer's "community" participates in how and where their food is grown. Every week throughout the season, the CSA community receives a box of that week's harvest. Most of the local CSAs will deliver to several convenient area locations, but they always encourage the community to come to the farm, and even to participate in the growing of their food.

cultivate: Process of breaking up the soil surface, removing weeds, and preparing for planting.

---

1. *Wikipedia*, s.v. "apiary." last modified January 2, 2017, *https://en.wikipedia.org/wiki/Apiary*.

farmers' market: A physical retail market featuring foods sold directly by farmers to consumers. Farmers' markets typically consist of booths, tables, or stands, outdoors or indoors, where farmers sell fruits, vegetables, meats, and sometimes prepared foods and beverages. They are distinguished from public markets, which are generally housed in permanent structures, open year-round, and offer a variety of nonfarmer/producer vendors, packaged foods, and nonfood products.

food desert: Geographic areas that lack convenient and affordable access to a range of healthy foods, including fruits, vegetables, whole grains, and high quality sources of protein.

food justice: Food justice is communities exercising their right to grow, sell, and eat healthy food. Healthy food is fresh, nutritious, affordable, culturally appropriate, and grown locally with care for the well-being of the land, workers, and animals.

food mileage: A term that refers to the distance food is transported from the time of its production until it reaches the consumer. Food miles are one factor used when assessing the environmental impact of food, including the impact on global warming.

gleaning: Gleaning is the act of collecting leftover crops from farmers' fields after they have been commercially harvested or on fields where it is not economically profitable to harvest. Some ancient cultures promoted gleaning as an early form of a welfare system.

glebe: Also known as church furlong, rectory manor, or parson's close, it is an area of land within an ecclesiastical parish used to support a parish priest.

guerrilla garden: Guerrilla gardening is the act of gardening on land that the gardeners do not have any legal rights to utilize, such as an abandoned site; an area that is not being cared for; private property. Guerrilla gardeners raise plants, frequently focusing on food crops or plants intended for aesthetic purposes. See also *seed bombs*.

hydroponics: The cultivation of plants by placing the roots in liquid nutrient solutions rather than in soil; soilless growth of plants.

Jubilee: The year at the end of seven cycles of *shmita* (sabbatical years), and according to biblical regulations it had a special impact on the ownership and management of land in Israel. Jubilee deals largely with land, property, and property rights. According to Leviticus, slaves and prisoners would be freed, debts would be forgiven, and the mercies of God would be particularly manifest during a Jubilee year.

Master Gardener: Master Gardener programs (also known as Extension Master Gardener Programs) are volunteer programs that train individuals in the science and art of gardening. These individuals pass on the information they learned during their training, as volunteers who advise and educate the public on gardening and horticulture.

100 Mile Bouquet: Not using flowers that have to fly on planes or travel from another hemisphere. See *https://slowflowers.com/*.

100 Mile Diet: Eating food products produced within a 100-mile radius of where the consumer lives. See also *food mileage.*

organic food: Food produced by methods that comply with the standards of organic farming. Standards vary worldwide, but in general these practices strive to cycle resources, promote ecological balance, and conserve biodiversity. Organizations regulating organic products may restrict the use of certain pesticides, fertilizers, irradiation, industrial solvents, or synthetic food additives.

permaculture: A basic concept that examines and follows nature's patterns that advocates designing human systems based on natural ecosystems. Defined by Bill Mollison, the creator of the term in the 1970s, "permaculture is a philosophy of working with, rather than against nature; of protracted and thoughtful observation rather than protracted and thoughtless labor; of looking at plants and animals in all their functions, rather than treading any area as a single-product system."[2]

pocket park: Empty lots that present impediments to future housing development are prime candidates for pocket parks. Through-lots, which connect neighborhoods and streets, are particularly appropriate, as they can serve as a means of pedestrian connection.

Sabbath: A time of rest; among Christians, Sunday is a day of rest and worship; in the Bible, it is the seventh day of the week observed from Friday evening to Saturday evening as a day of rest and worship. Its theological meaning is rooted in God's rest following the six days of creation (Gen. 2:2–3). In Leviticus 25:1–7, the sabbath year is when the land was to be at complete rest.

saints, patron and matron: *Saint Abigail:* Matron saint of beekeepers
Saint Dorothy: Matron saint of fruit tree growers and orchards
Saint Fiacre: Patron saint of herb and vegetable gardens and gardeners
Saint Patrick: Patron saint of organic gardening
Saint George: Patron saint of farmers

seed bombs: For starters, they are not explosive or edible. This is a little ball made up of a combination of compost, clay, and seeds. The compost and clay act

---

2. *www.heathcote.org/PCIntro/2WhatIsPermaculture.htm.*

as a carrier for the seeds so they can be launched over walls or fences and into inaccessible areas such as wastelands or railways. This is not an endorsement for seed bombing your diocesan office!

sustainability: The quality of not being harmful to the environment or depleting natural resources, and thereby supporting long-term ecological balance.

tilth: The physical condition of soil, especially in relation to its suitability for planting or growing a crop.

victory garden: Vegetable, fruit, and herb gardens were planted at private residences and public lands during World War I and World War II. They were used along with rationing stamps to reduce pressure on the public food supply. Besides indirectly aiding the war effort, these gardens were also considered a civil "morale booster" in that gardeners could feel empowered by their contribution of labor and rewarded by the produce grown, making victory gardens a part of daily life on the home front.

wild foraging: Items gathered growing wild in fields or woods. Can include ramps (wild leeks), dandelion greens, morel and puffball mushrooms, fiddlehead greens, wild asparagus, strawberries, blueberries, and a variety of nuts.

APPENDIX B

Brian's Seven Steps to a Successful Agrarian Ministry

1. **Network.** Once the light bulb clicks on in your head that you want to do something, start by sharing the idea with people who can share your enthusiasm. Stay away from Debbie and Donnie Downer. Your goal is to find a partner in crime. Start networking to find others in your congregation or community who share your interest and passion. God and Jesus are big on the idea of getting things going in groups:

   - "It is not good that the man should be alone." (Gen. 2:18)
   - "For where two or three are gathered in my name, I am there among them." (Matt. 18:20)
   - "And he called to him the twelve, and began to send them out two by two." (Mark 6:7)
   - And don't forget the Trinity!

2. **Dream.** Find an agrarian ministry nearby and contact the key stakeholders to see if they are willing to do a "show and tell" for you. If at all possible, do it at the garden, farm, or ministry. Stand in the middle of the garden and have them tell their story. Get all of your senses involved. Start with the Episcopal Asset Map[1] and click on community garden. Or do an Internet search with the following key words: church, community, garden, name of your town or surrounding area, and name of your faith community/ denomination. Develop a vision. While it might be stretching it a bit far to invoke Proverbs 29:18 (KJV), "Where there is no vision, the people perish," it is important to start by dreaming and putting your vision on paper.

3. **Plant.** While you are planning, recruiting, identifying assets to make it all happen, plant something! Maybe it is a radish seed in a paper cup. Or a small patch of wheat stuck in a corner. Or starting a pollinator garden in a weed-filled parking strip. Just plant something! Forgiveness is easier than permission. For needed inspiration, Google "Ron Finley Guerilla Gardener" and watch his TED talk.

4. **Ask.** Bring along key stakeholders: rector, vestry, outreach committee, flower guild, youth, and so on. Dollar to a donut, you will find multiple green thumbs that will want to climb on board and help you bring your dream to reality. A loose translation of James 4:3, "You have not because you ask not." Start asking for approval to "plow ahead": donation of garden tools, expert advice, plants to transplant, seeds, volunteers, drip irrigation, promotion, sponsorship, and financial support. And don't let people off the hook because they claim they have the opposite of a green thumb. Get them to help with the logistics, promotion, and baking cookies!

5. **Evangelize.** Don't hide your light under a bushel. While you want to make sure you have a sunny, level, and well-drained site that has access to water, you also want to make sure that people see it. Having a church garden in a conspicuous spot that can be seen by people passing by communicates the values of your congregation and reminds parishioners, coming and going, that they are welcome to be a part of your ministry. Make sure you have signage, so people know what you are up to.

6. **Share.** Be thoughtful as to what you are going to do with your food. Start a community garden where neighbors, especially those without yards, can have a plot to grow their own food. Or a church garden that grows food for community meals, local food banks, and feeding programs. Another option that is starting

---

1. *https://episcopalassetmap.org/.*

to catch on is selling food on Sundays between and after worship services, with the profit going to food programs locally or globally. St. John's, Lynchburg, Virginia, donates part of their sales to Episcopal Relief & Development for global programs that focus on hunger alleviation. They also support Lynchburg Grows, a community-wide initiative to restore a number of abandoned greenhouses for reuse as sources for food, education, and employment for those in need.

7. **Pray.** Make space for worship and spiritual reflection. Celebrate Rogation. Include a worktable that doubles as a communion table. Or a baptismal font that birds and bees can drink from. Consider the Rule of St. Benedict to love and appreciate our planet and reverence for all that God has created. As your hands get dirty and muscles ache, remember your work in the garden is a prayer, *ora et labora*.

APPENDIX C
Links and Ideas to . . .

Start a Garden

- Ten Steps to Starting a Community Garden
  *https://communitygarden.org/resources/10-steps-to-starting-a-community
  -garden/*
- Creating a Faith-Based Community Garden
  *http://sustainabletraditions.com/2010/04/creating-a-faith-based
  community-garden/*
- Starting a Community Garden
  *http://aggie-horticulture.tamu.edu/kindergarden/CHILD/COM
  /COMMUN.HTM*

Find Funding

- **United Thank Offering**—Known worldwide as UTO, the United Thank Offering grants are awarded for projects that address human needs and help alleviate poverty, both domestically and internationally in the Episcopal Church and the Anglican Communion. United Thank Offering was founded to support innovative mission and ministry that the Episcopal Church budget has not yet expanded to fund and to promote thankfulness and mission in the whole Church. The funds are not permitted for the continuation of ongoing ministries. *www.episcopalchurch.org/page/uto-grants*

- *Jubilee Ministry Grants*—One of the ways the Episcopal Church addresses domestic poverty is through its Jubilee network, which consists of over six hundred Jubilee Ministry Centers. These centers empower the poor and oppressed in their communities by providing direct services, such as food, shelter, and healthcare, and also by advocating for human rights. If your congregation or ministry is a Jubilee Ministry Center, you are eligible to apply for a *Jubilee Development Grant* or *Jubilee Impact Grant.* *www.episcopalchurch.org/library/office/jubilee-ministries*

- *Diocesan grants*—A growing number of dioceses offer grants for environmental initiatives. Check to see if your diocese offers any. For example: Vermont has the Alleluia Fund *http://diovermont.org/alleluia-fund.php*, Los Angeles has Seeds of Hope *http://seedsofhope.ladiocese.org*, Diocese of Olympia has the Bishop's Committee on the Environment *www.bce-ecww.org/*, and the Diocese of Rochester has mission grants *www.episcopalrochester.org/content/mission-grants*.

- *Government grants*—These are often offered by the state to increase the use of open space for agriculture that allows them to collect federal funding. Check with your state's environmental protection agency or county extension service for opportunities. Other options include

  - Beginning Farmers *www.beginningfarmers.org/funding-resources/*
  - US Department of Agriculture *www.ams.usda.gov/services/grants*
  - Office of Faith-Based and Neighborhood Partnerships at the USDA *www.usda.gov/wps/portal/usda/usdahome?navid=fbnp*

Work with Volunteers

- *Scheduling* *https://signup.com/*

- *Scouting*—Boy and Girl Scouts are always looking for places to do projects. Whether they are Cub Scouts or Brownies, or older scouts working on Eagle Projects or Gold Awards, your agrarian ministry might give them a place to work and grow.

  - *http://www.scouting.org/LocalCouncilLocator.aspx*
  - *http://www.girlscouts.org/en/about-girl-scouts/join/council-finder.html*

- *Community service*—Many high schools and colleges have community service requirements for their students. Contact your local schools, community colleges, and universities to seek volunteers.

Go Local

- Farmers' Markets
  https://farmersmarketcoalition.org/
  https://chicago-urban-agriculture.wikispaces.
  com/10.+How+to+Set+Up+a+Farmers+Market
- Food Pantries
  http://articles.bplans.com/how-to-start-a-food-pantry/

Get Connected

- Cultivate: Episcopal Food Movement
  www.facebook.com/EpiscopalFoodMovement/
- Christian Food Network
  www.churchwork.com/christian-food-movement/
- Asset-Based Community Development (ABCD)
  www.episcopalrelief.org/what-we-do/asset-based-community-development
- Called to Transformation
  http://calledtotransformation.org
- Asset Map of The Episcopal Church
  https://episcopalassetmap.org
- A Rocha
  https://arocha.us
- Urban Farming
  www.urbanfarming.org/

APPENDIX D

Featured Gardens, Farmers' Markets, and Food Pantries

Alabama

Camp McDowell, Nauvoo *http://mcdowellfarmschool.com*

Greene Street Market, Huntsville *www.greenestreetmarket.com*

Homegrown Alabama Farmers Market with Canterbury Episcopal Chapel, Tuscaloosa
www.facebook.com/homegrown.alabama/

Arizona

Good Shepherd Mission, Fort Defiance *www.goodshepmission.org*

Imago Dei Middle School, Tucson *www.imagodeischool.org/student-life/community-service*

California

The Abundant Table, Santa Paula *www.theabundanttable.org*

Camp Stevens *http://campstevens.org/property/*

The Cathedral of St. Paul, Los Angeles *www.cathedral-life.ladiocese.org*

Emerson Avenue Community Garden, Westchester *www.eacgc.org*

The Gooden School, Sierra Madre *www.goodenschool.org/page/46678_ServiceLearning.asp*

Holy Nativity, Westchester, California *www.holynativityparish.org/the-community
    -garden-at-holy-nativity/*

Honoré Farm and Mill, Healdsburg *http://honoremill.org*

Red Door Vineyard, Church of the Epiphany, Agoura Hills *http://reddoorvineyard.org*

Seeds of Hope (Diocese of Los Angeles) *http://seedsofhope.ladiocese.org*

St. Gregory of Nyssa Food Pantry, San Francisco *www.saintgregorys.org/the-food
    -pantry.html*

St. Margaret's School, San Juan Capistrano *www.smes.org/page/School-Garden?pk=80307
    &fromId=217910*

St. Matthew's School, Pacific Palisades (look under Program: Service Learning)
    www.stmatthewsschool.com

Colorado

St. John's in the Wilderness (Cathedral), Denver *www.sjcathedral.org/FaithInAction*

Connecticut

Camp Washington, Lakeside *www.campwashington.org*

Church of the Holy Advent, Clinton *www.holyadventclinton.org/About_Us/Mission_and
    _Outreach/Food-For-All-Garden/*

Community Gardens Ministry Network (Connecticut) *www.episcopalct.org/Find
    -Resources/ministry-networks/ministry-network-listing/*

Common Goods Garden, Old Saybrook *www.commongoodgardens.org*

Glebe House, Woodbury *www.glebehousemuseum.org*

Shoreline Soup Kitchen & Pantry, Old Saybrook *http://shorelinesoupkitchens.org*

St. Andrew's, Madison *www.standrewsmadison.org/noutreach.html*

St. James', West Hartford *http://stjameswh.org/mission/mission-commission/feeding-programs*

St. John's, Vernon *http://stjohnsvernonct.org/wrdp/?page_id=64*

St. Mark's, New Canaan *www.stmarksnewcanaan.org*

Trinity College, Hartford *www.trincoll.edu/NewsEvents/NewsArticles/pages/UrbanGarden 2012.aspx*

Trinity Retreat Center, West Cornwall *www.trinitywallstreet.org/about/archives/west-cornwall*

Georgia

Peachtree Road Farmers' Market, Atlanta *www.peachtreeroadfarmersmarket.com*

Haiti

Centre Diocesain de Development et de Secours *www.egliseepiscopaledhaiti.org*

St. Paul's School, Caracol *www.episcopalchurch.org/parish/st paul-caracol-haiti*

Hawaii

Camp Mokule`ia *http://campmokuleia.com/programs/navigating change-program/*

'Iolani School, Honolulu *www.iolani.org*

Honduras

Escuela Agricola Hogar de Amor y Esperanza, Talanga *http://escuelaagricolahogarde amoryesperanza.blogspot.com*

Illinois

St. Paul and the Redeemer, Chicago *www.sprchicago.org/food-garden/*

Iowa

St. Timothy's, West Des Moines *www.growthefood.org*

Kentucky

London Ferrell Community Garden, Lexington *https://transygardens.wordpress.com/about/*

Louisiana

Jericho Road, New Orleans *http://jerichohousing.org/investment/*

Saratoga Street Fruit Orchard, New Orleans *www.facebook.com/pages/Saratoga-Street -Fruit-tree-orchard/230353463729926*

Maine

Camp Bishopswood *http://campbishopswood.org*

Massachusetts

Emery House, Society of St. John the Evangelist, West Newbury *http://ssje.org/emery
ecology.html*

Michigan

Plainsong Farm, Rockford *http://plainsongfarm.com*

Minnesota

First Nations' Kitchen, Minneapolis *https://firstnationskitchen.org*

Missouri

Church of the Good Shepherd, Town and Country *http://goodshepherdec.org/outreach-2*

The Peace Meal Project, St. Louis *www.discoverstmark.org/ministries/missions/peace
-meal-project/*

New Jersey

The Healthier Heart Farmer's Market, Trenton *www.trinitycathedralnj.org/the-healthier
-heart-farmers-market.html*

New York

Bard College *http://inside.bard.edu/horticulture/maps/popups/community.html*

Bluestone Farm, Brewster *www.facebook.com/Bluestone-Farm-Fans-116453775039403
/?fref=ts&ref=br_tf*

Holy Cross Monastery, West Park *www.holycrossmonastery.com*

St. Hilda & St. Hugh High School, Manhattan *www.sthildas.org/page.cfm?p=759*

North Carolina

Episcopal Farmworker Ministry (Diocese of East Carolina and North Carolina) *www.
facebook.com/Episcopal-Farmworker-Ministry-257498467633231/*

Trinity Episcopal School, Charlotte *http://friendship-gardens.org/programs/garden-network/*

Ohio

Bellwether Farm *http://dohiocampandretreatfarm.com*

Good Earth Farm, Akron *https://commonfriars.wordpress.com*

Kenyon College *www.kenyon.edu/directories/offices-services/brown-family-environmental -center/news-information/newsletter-archive/newsletter-articles/welcome-to-the-wild life-garden/*

The Proctor Center *http://proctercenter.org/about-the-farm/*

Pennsylvania

St. Peter's in the Great Valley, Malvern *www.stpetersgv.org/who-we-are/about-our-sheep/*

South Carolina

Gravatt Farm at Camp Gravatt Camp and Conference Center, Aiken *www.campgravatt.org/ gravattfarms/*

Voorhees College, Denmark *www.voorhees.edu*

Tennessee

Calvary Episcopal Church, Memphis *www.calvarymemphis.org*

Church of the Annunciation, Cordova *www.episcopalcordova.org/sacred-grounds*

Colmore Farm (now St. Andrew's School), Sewanee *www.sasweb.org/page.cfm?p=528*

DuBose Memorial Church Training School, Monteagle *www.episcopalchurch.org /library/glossary/dubose-memorial-church-training-school-monteagle-tennessee*

Episcopal School of Knoxville *http://esknoxville.org*

Otey Memorial Parish, Sewanee *https://cacsewanee.wordpress.com*

Southern Province of the Sisterhood of St. Mary *http://stmary-conventsewanee.org*

St. Mary's Cathedral, Memphis *www.stmarysmemphis.org/article/st-marys-cathedral -neighborhood-garden/*

Thistle & Bee (Memphis & Cordova) *www.calvarymemphis.org/thistle-and-bee*

Thistle Farms, Nashville *www.facebook.com/ThistleFarms*

The University Farm, Sewanee *www.sewanee.edu/offices/oess/university-farm/*

Texas

Church of Our Saviour, Dallas *www.facebook.com/Our-Saviour-Community-Gardens -145994625415780/*

Gardeners in Community Development *www.gardendallas.org*

St. Mary Magdalene, Manor *www.facebook.com/iamsmm/*

Saint Michael's Farmers Market, Dallas *www.saintmichaelsmarket.com*

Utah

Homer Dale Community Farm, Bluff *www.navajoland.org/dfc/newsdetail_2/3169642*

Vermont

Grow Compost *www.facebook.com/compostvt/*

Rock Point Gardens Project, Burlington *www.rockpointgardens.org*

Virginia

Episcopal High School, Alexandria *www.episcopalhighschool.org/student_life
    /environmental-sustainability/index.aspx*

Glebe Church, Suffolk *www.facebook.com/GlebeChurchSuffolk*

St. Stephen's Farmers Market, Richmond *www.ststephensrva.org/community/farmers
    -market/*

Virginia Theological Seminary *www.missionalvoices.com/cultivate-vts-garden-tour/*

Washington

Bishop's Committee for the Environment, Diocese of Olympia *http://ecww.org/diocesan
    -ministries/committees-and-commissions/bishops-committee-for-the-environment/*

Church of the Holy Cross, Redmond *www.holycrossredmond.org/Ministries/FoodBankFarm*

St. Andrew's, Seattle *www.saintandrewsseattle.org/organic-vegetable-garden/*

St. Columba's Just Garden, Kent *www.stcolumbakent.org/service*

St. James, Kent *www.facebook.com/Kent-Community-Garden-64th-Ave-and-James-St
    -353229894776613/*

St. Mark's Cathedral, Seattle *www.saintmarks.org/saint-marks-urban-garden-bee-ministry*

APPENDIX E
Resources

Websites

Abundant Life Garden Project Curriculum *www.episcopalrelief.org/church-in-action
    /christian-formation/christian-formation-for-children*

American Community Garden Association *https://communitygarden.org/*

The Beecken Center of the School of Theology at the University of the South: Sewanee
    http://beeckencenter.sewanee.edu

Christian Food Movement *www.churchwork.com/christian-food-movement/*

Cultivate: Episcopal Food Network *www.facebook.com/EpiscopalFoodMovement/?fref=ts*

Earth Ministry *http://earthministry.org*

ECHO: Fighting World Hunger *www.echonet.org/*

Environmental Change-Makers *https://envirochangemakers.org*

Episcopal Aquaponics Experiment *www.facebook.com/episcopalaquaponics/*

Episcopal Relief and Development *www.episcopalrelief.org*

Genesis Covenant *www.episcopalchurch.org/posts/publicaffairs/genesis-covenant-and-green
-certification-means-energy-savings-episcopal*

Green Anglicans *http://acen.anglicancommunion.org/*

Green Burial Council *http://greenburialcouncil.org/*

Grow Compost of Vermont *www.growcompost.com*

Memphis Tilth *www.memphistilth.org/*

Plainsong Farm *http://plainsongfarm.com and www.facebook.com/PlainsongFarms/*

Seattle Tilth *www.seattletilth.org*

Seeds of Hope *http://seedsofhope.ladiocese.org*

Virginia Theological Seminary *www.missionalvoices.com/cultivate-vts-garden-tour/*

Wake Forest University School of Divinity: Food, Health, and Ecological Well-Being Program: *http://divinity.wfu.edu/*

Watershed Discipleship *https://watersheddiscipleship.org/*

Print

Bahnson, Fred. *Soil and Sacrament: A Spiritual Memoir of Food and Faith.* New York: Simon & Schuster, 2013.

Bahnson, Fred, and Norman Wirzba. *Making Peace with the Land: God's Call to Reconcile with Creation.* Downer's Grove, IL: InterVarsity Press, 2012.

Berry, Wendell. *The Art of the Commonplace: The Agrarian Essays of Wendell Berry.* Berkeley, CA: Counterpoint, 2002.

Davis, Ellen F. *Scripture, Culture, and Agriculture: An Agrarian Reading of the Bible.* New York: Cambridge University Press, 2009.

Hayden-Smith, Rose. *Sowing the Seeds of Victory: American Gardening Programs of World War I.* Jefferson, NC: McFarland & Company, 2014.

McDuff, Mallory. *Sacred Acts: How Churches Are Working to Protect Earth's Climate.* Gabriola Island, British Columbia: New Society Publishers, 2012.

Miles, Sara. *Jesus Freak: Feeding Healing Raising the Dead.* San Francisco: Jossey-Bass, 2010.

———. *Take This Bread: A Radical Conversion.* New York: Ballantine Books, 2008.

Myers, Ched. *Watershed Discipleship: Reinhabiting Bioregional Faith and Practice*. Eugene, OR: Wipf and Stock, 2016.

Schut, Michael. *Food & Faith: Justice, Joy, and Daily Bread*. New York: Morehouse, 2009.

Sine, Christine. *To Garden with God*. Seattle, WA: Mustard Seed Associates, 2009.

Stevens, Becca. *Snake Oil: The Art of Healing and Truth-Telling*. New York: Jericho Books, 2013.

Sutterfield, Ragan. *Farming as a Spiritual Discipline*. Indianapolis, IN: Doulos Christou Press, 2009.

Willis, Laura Lapins. *Finding God in a Bag of Groceries: Sharing Food, Discovering Grace*. Nashville: United Methodist Publishing House, 2013.

Wirzba, Norman. *Food & Faith: A Theology of Eating*. New York: Cambridge University Press, 2011.

Wirzba, Norman, and Barbara Kingslover. *The Essential Agrarian Reader: The Future of Culture, Community, and the Land*. Louisville: University Press of Kentucky, 2003.